Poems, Maxims &
Extended Thoughts

Dr. Chriss Warren Foster

Kendall Hunt
publishing company

Cover image © Malik Seneferu

Kendall Hunt
p u b l i s h i n g   c o m p a n y

www.kendallhunt.com
Send all inquiries to:
4050 Westmark Drive
Dubuque, IA 52004-1840

Copyright © 2016 by Kendall Hunt Publishing Company

ISBN 978-1-5249-0411-1

Printed in the United States of America

DEDICATED TO THE WILD BUNCH

Nina, Kristopher, Nathan, Kien, Josiah Ra,
Nkosi, and Njua Obasi

Contents

CHAPTER TWO: THE MAXIMS . . . 21

CHAPTER THREE: EXTENDED THOUGHTS . . . 59

Preface

Two essential skills required for success in any professional endeavor are reading and writing, and these skills are often quite difficult to hone in preparation for college writing courses, especially for the writing of essays and lengthy research assignments that require the use of a specified style when past experiences of primary and secondary education are riddled with obstacles both external and self-imposed. Students of today's world have grown accustomed to brevity in communication using texting, Instagram®, Snapchat®, and other messaging apps yet to be introduced. This is not a problem for students already skilled in switching from one form of coded language to another, as they can easily move from abbreviated language to formal Standard English. However, in the rush to keep oppressed students in a state of oppression, no viable, substantial effort is made to challenge, give voice, or respect the experiences and the rich background knowledge they bring to classrooms; if this were not the case, the widening abyss in levels of achievement would be quite narrow by now. *Poems, Maxims & Extended Thoughts* provides the means to segue into creativity, to open doors with reasons to write by presenting writing to respond to and challenges to readers to prompt them to demonstrate movement from narrative to argument structures.

Educators must acknowledge that students whose lives afford opportunities for consistent, uninterrupted education can and will succeed at much higher rates than those students made to face major stressors, stressors that no matter what intentions these students may have regarding their academic futures can interrupt without warning, producing major obstacles that thwart all efforts to engage in progressive work. Without appropriate support systems, these students will give in, become disillusioned, and thus lose the opportunity to achieve; all students need encouragement and assistance to reach their goals.

The written word whether poetry, fiction, or nonfiction is about a culmination of subjects—the lives that people are living or have lived (real or imagined), about people who are similar or different, about people who have something to share regarding their lives, their characters' lives and worlds; about the world and people's thoughts and opinions; and, most importantly, about persuasion and influence. Herein, readers are afforded endless opportunities to examine, evaluate, compare, respond to, and argue in support of or against outcomes. *Poems, Maxims & Extended Thoughts* is about life, and in this respect life is the inkwell from which the writings are drawn.

Dr. Chriss Warren Foster
May 2016

Introduction

Artwork by Karen Seneferu. Photo ©2016 Akil Foster.

Students in the process of honing writing skills after struggling through primary and secondary educational experiences often present barely having scratched the surface of their abilities and creative potential, and as such they lack the skills needed to complete coursework above average expectations, so they are often met with major issues in college classrooms. English may be a second, third, or even fourth language, so the struggle is exponential in a first-year composition course. Initially, students may be given multiple choice, placement tests to assess reading and writing skills, tests that do not always result in the correct "placement" in courses conducive to the resolution of learning deficits. Second, wherever the outcome of the assessment "places" these students, there is no guarantee that skilled, well trained educators are available to assure achievement of proficiency. Thus, the high school experience may be repeated. Third, once in designated classrooms, self-doubt often ensues with students questioning their abilities to read, comprehend, write well, and meet the immediate challenge to achieve at the same level as peers. Students often do not recognize or embrace their own value, and so they are easily discouraged. Through their attempts to complete writing assignments, students are shown that their writing skills are poor by way of low grades, and suggestions are made regarding the need for improvement, and yet over time little or no improvement is achieved—something is missing. Fourth, students are often met with educators who have preconceived notions about their abilities to achieve based on surnames, ethnicity, race, gender, skin color, and, of course, "placement." Students are also often met with resistance from educators who refuse to advocate for them, refuse to share all that they know will certainly lead these students to success.

What must students do to secure their academic futures? In this world where nothing is promised, it is easy to lose footing and fall over the edge into the abyss of failure. But if students can master the strength it takes to stabilize themselves every time the earth moves under their feet (attacked by microaggressions or countertransferences); if they can control and calm the angry tides of frustration that occasionally rise up inside of them for want of voice and self-expression; if they can speak to the depth of their feelings after facing the pain of failure and wearing smiles as shields; if they can see themselves as participants and contributors in the processes of their own lives and education; if they can learn to respond to life through their words (written and oral communication) and respect the power of written words; and, if they can wrestle themselves free of the binding attitudes and perceptions that others may have and hold against them, only then can they realize their highest levels of potential. Responding to life through words and actions promotes the power of written language; the symbolic pen flows with language from a deep well of thought. This book is a process from beginning to end wherein writing has occurred, a culmination of time, space, purpose, and permission to write.

POEMS, MAXIMS & EXTENDED THOUGHTS

The Poems

MESSENGERS

The Creator sends messengers into our lives.
They travel across worlds, great bodies of water,
And dry and treacherous lands to reach us.
Feeling our pain, they are drawn to and
Determined to reach us against all possible adversities.
Facing insurmountable obstacles they persist,
Coming with words of wisdom,

They pray silently for our health,
Hope, and happiness to be secured in the name of
The Creator.

They anoint us with life giving oils
Drawn from the cosmos and the earth.
They know the face behind the smile.
They hear the tears falling behind the laughter.
They know when we lose the ability to ask for help.
They come to heal.
When they come, you will know.

HOWLING AT THE MOON

I howled at the moon.
Resounding wails pierced the universe,
My locs stood on end,
There was no wind.

I howled at the moon.
The sky rained in response,
Drenching the earth,
Uprooting trees.

I howled at the moon.
The thundering of my heart,
Within my chest,
Awakened me.
The earth quaked.

I howled at the moon.
Crowds of life rushed
Into my existence,
Taking all that I had to give, and then
Walking away,
Looking back, laughing.
"Poor fool; she didn't know
Who we were."

I Howled at the moon,
After all, I learned,
but had not known that you,
Thought I, was a fool.

Angry, now,
I screamed at the moon,
"Come back, there's another part of my face
You haven't stepped on yet!"
And you all came and stepped
On my face . . . again and again,
And each time,
I grew stronger.

And now, holding the rain and
The power of the quaking earth,
In my locs and in my hands;
One sweeping motion,
Washes you and your footprints away,
The pain and frustration dissipate, immediately.

USE ME NO MORE MY BROTHERS

Use me no more my brothers,
My love is enclosed in a brown paper bag,
Tossed in the midst of a brief "Good-bye."
I cannot be reached.
I am disconnected.
My feelings are closed.
I am no longer home.

I wiped tears,
And soothed pain, but
No one was there for
My tears,
My pain.
Use me no more my brothers.
My love is enclosed in a brown paper bag,
Tossed in the midst of a brief "Good-bye."

YELLOW LEAVES

Bright, beautiful yellow leaves,
Under foot
On the cracked sidewalk
After a light fall rain
In West Oakland
Symbolic of
Trampled potential.

COMMUNICATION

Communication is asked for,
But is it ever truly given?

Telling all that one feels,
All that one hopes and dreams for,
In the moment,
Words that fall on
Ears that try, but
Cannot receive the depth of it all.

Letting go, not expecting anything in return,
To avoid disappointment
To acknowledge that no one thinks or feels
Exactly the same way
About a thing, expression, or situation.

Communication is easy to ask for, but
Oh so difficult to deliver.

IMAGES

Looking out into the darkness of the night,
I followed the pattern of the dark and angry clouds.
And then I noticed my reflection in the window,
A tremendous weight pressed heavy on my chest.
The clouds intuited my troubles.
Suddenly, it began to rain.

MARK

Mark is the only little man I know
Whose dimples
Touch my soul and
Give me hope.

WRITING

Words written on a page
Serve an important purpose.
They are the thoughts and feelings
That pour from the mind and metaphoric heart,
And flow through the fingers,
To reach the eyes,
Ears, and hearts
And minds of those
Who have not yet trusted
Their fingers to handle such
Precious cargo.

OLDER, BUT NOT WISER

I find myself back
In the same relationship,
A relationship that did not work,
The first time,
The second time, and
Now, the third time;
I am a
Revolving door

WHAT WERE YOU SAYING?

I didn't hear you,
I was busy
Wondering what
You were whispering to

That person over there
When you thought I
Wasn't paying attention, so
What were you saying?

LISTENING AND HEARING (MAKING CONNECTIONS)

I didn't understand when you said,
"I *do* love you," as if you were
Answering a question
That I did not ask, or
Trying to convince
Yourself that there was
Truth and honesty in
The words.

I didn't understand when you said, coarsely
And abruptly,
"Don't call me . . . *I'll get back to you.*"
Sending a message,
That I apparently did not want to, or
Could not hear.

I didn't understand when you said,
"I love you. *I don't want to lose you,*"
When all the while
You were pushing me away.

I didn't understand when you said,
"You can't give me what I need,"
When I know that I gave you all that you asked for,
And more.

After some time alone, I
Emerged from my self-imposed,
Confused state of mind and
Blind-Love coma.

DD THE BAG BOY

He always came with his bag,
His stuff,
Everything he needed.
But he never stayed the whole night.

ONLY IF . . .

If he did not have such a great smile,
An exceptional physical presence,
And the ability to make me feel . . .
And the potential for such greatness;

If he would just stop calling me,
Being in my presence,
Causing me to feel . . .
And showing me his potential to be a good husband

If he were not so young and old,
At the same time

If I did not need him,
Love him, so much,
I could let this go.

NOT AGAIN!

So, you're not speaking to me again,
I knew it was coming.
When you were just a child,
And I said no,
You would pout for hours, days, weeks,
Until I gave in because
I could not live without your smile
And you knew it.

But you are grown now.
Even if you refuse to acknowledge it,

You *are* grown.
And no means no
The memories of your smile will suffice.

DISCIPLINE NOT TAKEN LIGHTLY

You say that your Mom spanked you
Because you were not being
A good boy?
Well, what can I say, baby?

If you know what you did, and
Why she did what she did,
You have all of the knowledge required
To assure that you never
Get spanked again. Right?

SO YOU'RE MARRIED . . . HOW ABOUT THAT?

When I found out that you belonged to someone else
I was angry, and when I recovered,
I could not wait to see you again.
This is not okay.

And seeing you was the best time
The best time in a long time
A long time coming,
A long time until the next time,
No, I do not care what anyone thinks.

Watching you sleep
Reminds me of how closed you are
Reminds me that you did not reveal yourself
Reminds me that I can never know all of you
Reminds me that I may not want to know
Reminds me that reality is
Not always so important
In the moment.

THE BEST KISSES

Wet, juicy
Soft, smooth
Tasty,
Yours

MAKING LOVE IS NOT A FIGHT

Unless what one is giving
One really wants to maintain
For oneself.
Narcissist?
In the midst of the splendor
You ask, "Is this what you want,"
I answer in my head
"Yes, but only if you really want me to have it."

THE TELEGRAPHED NOTE

On Wednesday of last week, three masked pigs,
Two goats, nine geese, and two pugs
Broke into the local Whole Foods® market
And stole a grocery basket filled with frozen pizza pies,
Two six packs of beer,
And three bottles of Neutrogena® oil . . . [at the end the translation was]
Three strippers stole a six-pack of beer.

BLANK CARD

Time passes, and
The seeds we sow
Sink down into the earth and bear fruit, or
Disperse into the wind, carried
Who knows where.
But alas,
All is not lost.
Friendships do develop.
Be well, my love.

PROMISES

I will not cry at sad movies.
I will not yearn for warmth.
I will not fear being alone, sleeping alone.
I will forgive myself for believing in you.
I will remove the abstract noun "love" from
My vocabulary, my heart, my brain,
My intuitive spirit, so that
I will not feel.
I will not listen for the sound of your voice.
I will not look for you in a crowd.
I will not feel your breath against the back of my neck.
I will not, I cannot, I will force myself not to care.
I promise!

TORN UP

Speaking, but not making sense;
Listening, but not hearing;
Hungry, but not seeking food;
Staring, but not seeing;
Wanting answers, but not asking questions;
Thinking, but not reaching conclusions;
Laughing, when nothing is funny,
And crying for no apparent reason;
These are the signs.

SADNESS

"Sadness is a funning thing,"
I hear people say that all of the time, but
I don't get it.

I NEVER THOUGHT THAT I . . .

I never thought that I
Would be that

"Angry Sista"
[Definition: a phrase used by Black men
Who are in denial
about their contributions
to the outcome]
I was too intelligent,
And far too mature.

I never thought that I
Would project ill will
And misfortune
Onto anyone.
I was too loving,
Too forgiving.

I never thought that I would feel,
The way that I feel
Right now.

But then,
I never thought,
That I would ever meet someone
Like you.

LESSONS LEARNED

I insist on being alone,
Angry, upset, and confused
At this time.

I am satisfied like this,
I am focused,
I can get things done, and if asked
I can identify what is bothering me.

When the pain subsides, and
I return as a new self,
I will think clearly,
Give nothing,

Believe nothing,
And never trust anyone.

YOU LIED

To lie is to be untruthful.
You lied,
When you told me
Who you were, but
I forgive you
Because even you
Did not know
Who you were.

THANK YOU!

Thank you for the hurt,
It has strengthened me.

Thank you for the persistent pain,
It has strengthened me.

Thank you for upsetting my existence,
It has strengthened me.

Thank you for bringing back the emptiness
That was missing for so long,
The emptiness I thought had gone away . . . forever,
When I met you,
It has strengthened me.

Thank you for allowing me to make a fool
Of myself one last time,
It has strengthened me.

Thank you for allowing me to understand
Your purpose in my life;
I am stronger now than ever before

Just in case someone like you
Comes along, again.

STUDY HABITS

There is a time
Among the seconds, minutes
And hours of the day
When you will do your best
Work, and
Gain the most from reading,
Writing, studying.
Find the time
Best suited for you.

IF I EVER CROSS YOUR MIND

If I ever cross your mind,
Please do not call me,
I am busy healing.

I, on the other hand,
Will think of you every day,
Until the sky turns silver,
Until fish walk on land,
Until . . .

If I ever cross your mind,
Please let the thought be brief,
I might feel you.

If I ever cross your mind,
Remember that I loved you,
That I love you . . .
That loving you
Is the last . . .
Was the last opportunity
I allowed myself
To love.

If I ever cross your mind,
Cancel the thought quickly,
I will know that I
Have crossed your mind, and
The wound will open, and
I just might bleed,
To death.

HELLO . . . ?

I don't know why I called,
I don't know what
Is appropriate here,
I can't find words.
I am without speech.

I do know that I will miss talking to you,
Spending time
With you . . . there is no point in this,
I am empty.
"Good-bye."

YOU ASKED . . .

You asked, and I could not explain
The depth of my feelings.
I wondered if even I knew
What I really meant.

In your presence, I am all
That I believe I
Can be.
Without you,
I wonder.

WHEN

When I grow up, I want to be
A great force like the ocean.
When I grow up, I want to be
As strong as an angry, ebbing tide.

When I grow up,
How will I know?
Will you be there to tell me?

I LOVE

I love because that's what my parents taught me, modeled
For me; I live because The Creator lets me live;
I learn because gifts and the capacity to do so
Were given to me; and,
I am hurting now because I am vulnerable and
Because I, mistakenly, gave you
My heart.

TRUTHS: I CAN'T COME TO CLASS TODAY . . .

My mother died,
My aunt died,
My father died,
My uncle died,
My Grandmother died.
My brother was shot,
My brother was killed,
My boyfriend was shot, and
He died in front of my house.
I have to see a counselor,
I am not enrolled in this class, yet,
I am having a kidney transplant,
I lost my baby last night.
My visa expired; I will be deported today . . .
The struggle is real.

Exercise   1

EXERCISE WORKSHEET FOR SMALL GROUP
DISCUSSION AND FIRST WRITING ASSIGNMENT

PART I: Select four poems and list the titles here:

1. _____

2. _____

3. _____

4. _____

Preparation for discussion: For each poem selected, write a brief reflection, answering the following questions (use additional paper if necessary):
a) What is the subject?
b) Who is speaking?
c) What is the tone of the poem?
d) What is happening?
e) What is your interpretation of the poem?
f) How does each poem make you feel?

1.

The Maxims

Photo ©2016 Akil Foster

METAPHOR

The enduring symbolism of the "Bus Ride"
Looms large, unattended,
Over every Black family's threshold,
And the lives of Black children.

HEALING

Healing is the result of
Acquiring the ability
To let go of the things
That caused internal damage
To one's soul.

IF

If you had only allowed yourself
To get to know
Who I am,
You would still be here,
With me.

EXCUSES

Excuses are the reasons we give
For not accomplishing
What we know we can accomplish
If we put forth the effort to do so.

THE QUESTION

Be careful when asking someone a question like,
"What do you want from me?"
The person being asked does not have the answer.
What is desired cannot yet be known, so
It is best not to ask because a random answer thought of
In the moment, will lead to an attempt to try to do or be it.
What? Exactly!

PHENOMENOLOGY – " . . . GETTING BACK TO THE THINGS THEMSELVES" (HUSSERL)

So what is the structure of the experience of things that our quivering
    sensibilities
Do not allow us to speak aloud?
Moments when we are embarrassed, confused, confronted, shocked.
Moments when the words or actions imposed upon us through
language and culture are not enough,
Moments when we hold things inside for want of expression
Moments when epiphanies awaken us,
But we are silenced.
The essence of existence,
Waiting to be tapped,
Waiting to rise to the surface and shout . . . this is what it *was* like,
What it *is* like for *me* to experience _____,
Only you can fill in the blank and narrate the depth of it.

SITTING STILL IS OFTEN THE BEST COURSE OF ACTION

Frustrated about life and things.
Can't make sense of people and their actions.
Can't get people to think like you do,
To work as hard as you do
Feeling like you are about to implode.
Looking for someone to tell,
Someone who will understand and
Take your side?
Sit still and breathe deeply
Those people do not exist.
If they did, you would not be
Experiencing things,
As they are.

OUTSOURCING CONTRIBUTES TO POVERTY AND HUNGER IN AMERICA

Through the back door, people repeat the mantra "jobs are being stolen
From Americans," but how can jobs be stolen, when someone in America
Is doing the hiring to assure that nannies are available to care for children,
That workers are available to harvest crops, and to assure that laborers will
Work for pennies on the dollar.

Americans are the ones taking advantage of a people whose goals are to
Support their families; lead better lives, to educate their children.
The hardest most loyal workers,
That Americans continue to employ,
While declaring "We must build a wall."

Beware of those who speak the loudest.
The ones outsourcing work for their corporations through the front door,
Taking jobs from Americans to avoid paying
Taxes, medical care, pensions, *a living wage.*
They seek cheap labor,
The same cheap labor, coming through the back door.
The place where they claim, "We must build a wall."

Americans live in poverty, struggle to find jobs,
Struggle to feed their families and children.
Americans control, poverty, joblessness, and
The outsourcing front door, as well as the
Outsourcing back door where, "We must build a wall."
Really?

LOST IN HERE

People do not understand depression until they experience it.
People say, "Oh, you'll be alright; get some exercise."
Or, they say, "Get over it."

They do not understand what it is like
To be in a room that seems to be shrinking,
To experience breathing in fresh air

That is suffocating,
To fear that the next breath will be
The last breath.

They do not know what it is like to feel one's
Throat suddenly becoming dry, and then closing.
To panic and tremble all over, for no apparent reason
To be thrust into a severe state of fear
Hyperventilation
Profuse sweating.
At these moments,
Lost inside one's body,
Reaching out for help.

WHERE I LIVE

Where I live,
I hear gunshots and delayed sirens.
I am not numb to the fear of random
Bullets piercing the walls of the house that
I live in
Trying to kill me.
I cannot play outside for fear of
Drive-by-shootings.

I cannot run races in the park
For fear of being arrested for an
Unknown crime, or for "looking like" someone who
May have committed a crime.
I can easily be killed.
I do not expect to live long.

Where I live,
My parents and their friends use drugs.
Any day now, I may be sold into prostitution
Because my parents need money.
I know only one world, so although
I am willing to abide by their wishes.
Secretly, I hope that someone will help me,

Save me, but no one can see me.
I am invisible.

I go to school, sometimes, but
My school does not welcome me, and
No one cares whether my homework is done,
No one cares whether I show up,
If I am missing,
No one comes looking for me.
I do not know what to expect.

Where I live,
It is peaceful and quite.
Sometimes raccoons scamper away when they
See me running through the yard.
Sometimes a deer will approach and enjoy the saltlick by the front door.
Sometimes wild turkeys corner the UPS truck, and I
Come to the rescue, throwing rocks to
Distract them.

I can play outside on the lawn,
Walk my dog, and go on hikes with friends.
I can play outside until the sun goes down.
I look forward to college, and
I have parents and teachers who believe in me.
I am met with few challenges in life,
But when challenges arise,
I am well prepared to handle them
With excellent support systems
My future is clear and bright.

Where I live,
My parents travel all over the world,
And I am left with nanny
She lives here too.
She always lets me do whatever I want.

Although I am not supposed to, I especially like sneaking
Into my dad's trophy room where all of the weapons
Are polished and displayed.
I know where he hides the key, so

POEMS, MAXIMS & EXTENDED THOUGHTS

Whenever my parents are away, and nanny
Is busy with my sister, I sneak into the
Trophy room, unlock the case, and
Handle any weapon I choose.

My father hunts wild game
And brings their heads home. I love
Hearing the stories of the "kill"
I see the way his eyes light up when he
Retells the stories of tracking and shooting
His prey and how powerful it made him feel.
 I want to feel like that too.

SEARCHING

Your coming into my life helped me find myself.
I felt the wholeness of self in such a profound way that
I thought maybe if you left, I would lack something.
I was not certain that I could survive, but I knew, cognitively
That love is in the mind, not in the heart.
There is no such thing
As a broken heart
Only a broken mind.

NO APPRECIATION? SO WHAT?

It takes a while to shed the skin that makes you
Think that you are obligated to please other people
Encountered in life,
No matter how they treat you.

On the job where your hard work is not
Acknowledged because your coworker is a close friend
Of the bosses', who not only sees his level of error,
But corrects and covers for him.
But who is to know?

Any effort you make
To expose him

Will fall back on you
Making *you* the
Hater.

Do your best work
Maintain a professional attitude
Leave the small, petty arguments to them.
Let them wallow in their own madness
While you prepare to
Move on.

FOR THE CHILDREN

One life, that's the promise,
Whether short or long.
On this earth, in this time
Choose wisely.

MAYBE IT'S THE WIND

Do you ever get that sensation, you know?
The one that makes you shiver
Uncontrollably, for a second, or two,
And you can't explain it?
Well, it might be a whisper,
A thought trying
To reach you, or
Maybe it's just the wind.

SITTING ACROSS THE TABLE

Sitting across the table,
I attempt to be a team player
When I know that I can never be
A part of your team.

I do not look like you,
I do not think like you,
I do not perceive you, as you perceive me.

You smile when I comment,
But there is hate in your eyes,
Your demeanor,
Between your teeth.
It oozes out when you speak kind words
That you do not mean.

I know that you attack
When I am not looking,
I know that you lead the
Invisible group
That works to
Undermine me.
You smile, and I see the lie
Behind the smile
that shows
The sinister nature
Of your soul.

SORRY

"Sorry" is an adjective that no one should ever
Be compelled to use, unless he or she is truly
Sorrowful, but usually the intention
Is to do whatever was done all over again, that thing
That caused the adjective to be appended to the excuse
In the first place.

BROTHERS

In the neighborhoods where strength and swagger rule
And where the signs determine the turf,
You can decide whether there is honor and value
In living by the rule of survival that means
Taking your brother's life, or
Selling deadly substances to your sister.

COLD SHOULDER

A cold shoulder can turn
When you least expect it.
Its purpose is to let you know,
That your presence is no longer required.

A LOVING MOTHER AND WIFE

A loving mother loves unconditionally.
She does what she has to do, is charged to do,
And what she thinks is best;
She is often a misunderstood life force.

She makes sacrifices,
She lives in a state of persistent tension,
Sometimes while empty-armed and emotional,
She gives until she is worn out from loving,
Understanding, accepting empty apologies,
Holding in words that silently kill her,
Needing, wanting, and going without
All for the sake of children, and
A husband who will all
Leave her, eventually.

ENLIGHTENMENT

Enlightenment is acknowledgement of
The things you already knew,
But refused to accept.

MOMMY

The years have changed you so much that I
Hardly recognize you.
We can't talk much because your ability to hear,
Is so poor.
We can't go shopping like we used to because

POEMS, MAXIMS & EXTENDED THOUGHTS

Walking is so painful for you.
I feel you slipping away from me.
And then the moment comes when you laugh aloud, and
Your laughter returns you to me.
Following the laughter,
You can hear me, clearly
And the pace of your walking
Quickens.

DEFIANCE

We know all of the answers
At age twelve.
We are convinced that no one can possibly know
What we are going through, as if
Our parent were never twelve years old.

We decide how our lives should be run.
We become farsighted and wise though we know nothing of the world.
We can manipulate our own world, our friends, and our younger siblings.
We fall into an interminable abyss of attitude.
And when we fail, we place the blame on others.

If we are loved enough and our parents are strong enough,
We learn to scrutinize our peers, and make better decisions.
We learn that we have choices.

And if our parents and siblings are patient and tolerant, as
We make mistakes, entrap ourselves, and
Fight every attempt that is made to save us from ourselves,
By the grace of The Creator alone we will survive.

After lessons are learned and recorded,
Wounds are healed, and relationships are mended,
We grow into our adult lives, and
We ultimately become parents.

When our own children reach the age of twelve, and our self-imposed
Amnesia attempts to dissuade us,

To prevent the essential memory or our own behavior, but fails,
We reluctantly recognize ourselves, and
We painfully understand and accept the frustration, and pray.

WILDERNESS

I turned and looked into the face of the devil.
He glared at me, threatened to destroy me.
He spoke in a tongue that I could not comprehend.
He tormented my soul.
I sought to destroy him, to
Remove him from my world.
I had seen his face before,
Distorted, dark, scaled hues of red, pink, and green,
Now you wear his mask.

WHILE YOU SLEPT

I used to lightly stroke your cheek while you slept
And think about you snug in yellow pajamas,
Comfortable and warm and satisfied,
A stomach filled with breast milk.
Your first truck could never compete with the saucepan and spoon
That you preferred and used,
To make such a racket – your own music.

No lullaby was better than the music of Miles or Coltrane.
You did not need company to create and converse because
You allowed sounds to capture and nourish you.

I used to rush to your crib often during the night
To make sure, that you were still breathing, and now?
Now I stroke your head in my thoughts
And wonder whether you are still breathing.

GRANDMOTHER

"It's okay to eat that mud, it's God's mud"
I learned that the taste of life is often muddied
By prejudice, hate, and failure,
But it is the food that we must ingest,
To arrive at an understanding of what is lacking,
In the world - equality, love, and success for all people.

Whatever ailed me, you healed me with
Oils and herbs drawn from the earth
Sitting in your presence, I was protected and loved.
Although you left this earth a long time ago,
I still need you.

I get wounded now and then, and
The memory and force of your love provide the salve that heals.
I remember thinking, how tall you were
And how much I yearned to be so tall.
You were only 4 feet 11 inches in height.
But you were a giant to me, and
I will never stand as tall as you.

The first time I saw you cry, I was packing up to
Move away, and you said,
"I'll never see you again."
But I was too busy to allow myself to understand
That you meant what you were saying.
I was too busy to know that you knew
That it was time for you to let me go,
Time for me to stand on my own two feet.

I was too busy to stop and acknowledge that
Your work was done – here on earth.
That is *the message* I missed.

But you left me with many
Useful tools such as the ability to love and
Understand people despite themselves, to be intuitive,
To move on when staying is useless, to persevere and survive,

---

To educate myself and to share that education with others,
To teach and influence, to walk through storms unafraid.

Although I am fairly certain that you are
Assisting God in some magnificent way,
Please look down here occasionally, if you will so that you can
See me, walk with me and touch my soul, and even speak to me
Because I am not afraid to hear your voice.
I miss you.

DAUGHTER

Remember that cashmere sweater that
You had to have, or you would
Have died?
Two days after the novelty wore off,
I found it crumpled on the floor, behind your bedroom door.
Remember when you glared at me in silence, and I asked,
"What's wrong, baby?"
But you would not say,
And ran away soon after?
And years went by,
And things changed,
And you finally told me,
And my life was changed forever.
But my pain was secondary
Because you had been hurting the whole time.

CUTTING LOSSES AND MOURNING

Take life seriously.
Understand that things do not always
Work the way one plans them.
Give freely and let go.
And when you get tired of dreaming,
Learn how to say, "No!"

TIME

I worked, and worked, and worked,
Everyone suffered.
I look back and see clearly
Why everyone suffered.
I sought higher education.
I earned enough money to take care of everyone.
And me?
Oh, I suffered too.
But time will mend us all.

TO LIVE

In order to live,
One must be alive.
It is impossible to do one
Without the assistance of the other.

THE HUG

The hug you ask for,
I can no longer give.
It got lost somewhere between, "Don't call me,"
And, "I don't want to see you."

PUGS

If you want a companion that you can count on, one
Who will not disagree or argue,
Who will always be glad to see you,
Who may not follow every command, but
Will listen attentively,

If you want a companion
Who will understand your need for empathy.
Stay up late
And never complain about

How long it takes you to
Finish a project, movie, or long hot bath.
Buy a pug.

TURTLES

Turtles should come with a warning label
That clearly states the following:
"Turtles cannot swim in the whirlpool
Of a flushing toilet"
Turtles should only be given to
Children capable of reading.

APATHY USA

Here in the city of Apathy,
I have a lot of company.
The Do Nothings, Say Nothings, and
Want Nothings all live here, and
They never communicate with
The See Nothings, Hear Nothings, and Feel Nothings.
We have no desire to talk about Something,
And we don't care to know Anything.

JUDAS KISS

I did not know what
A Judas kiss was
Until you kissed
My cheek
And marked me

LIFE

Standing on the edge
Looking down at
Giant redwood trees

POEMS, MAXIMS & EXTENDED THOUGHTS

That resemble matchsticks,
I think that it is you I am placing my faith in.
But as I walk sideways
Across a sheer cliff,
I know it is The Creator
Who keeps me
From falling
Over the edge.
As I stand on the edge of life,
Placing one foot
In front of the other,
If I waiver unable to keep my balance
And fall off,
It's on me

INSENSITIVE

Understanding that
What you do
Can and will
Hurt others
Is to acknowledge
Your insensitivity.

GENERATION X

Pay close attention to the "X"
Malcolm explained exactly what it meant.
You have lost, ignored, blocked out
The message: He stumbled and fell
Before he realized who he was too.

Study the road that Malcolm traveled.
Learn what was revealed to him, and then
Wear the "X" with pride.
Affect change wherever you go,

And please,
Allow yourself to go somewhere,
Other than the grave . . . too soon.
Fill your head with knowledge,
Hold fast to that which you can control,
Yourself.

MICROAGGRESSIONS

Why am I just sitting here, now?
What happened?
Was it something the professor said?
Oh, I get it,
It was the word
That
Jumped
Out of the text
And
Assaulted me.

The words,
The images,
The looks,
The dismissals,
The intentional or unintentional
Acts that cut and disable.

RESISTANCE

Knowing that what you know is
Essential, but purposefully
Withholding it, unwilling
To pass the "knowing" on
To your students, is resistance.

WHEN STUDENTS TUNE OUT

We do not need a survey.
We do not need an assessment.
We need to look inside and reassess
Our goals and objectives for
Teaching.

Hypervigilance will enable one
To capture and remedy
The glazing over of the eyes,
Which is a moment when real
Teaching can return the wandering mind
To the classroom
Not embarrass,
Not shame, but
Recall the student
Reengage the students.
Ask "Where have you gone?"

MOVEMENT

How does one define movement?
Physical,
Fluid,
Dancing, walking, growing;
To ascend or descend;
Mentally,
Deepening one's understanding,
Enabling one to progress
From one state of being
To another.

FEET

When we first discover these short, stubby,
Extensions of ourselves,
We have no idea what they are,

And we cannot know how precious they really are,
Until we can no longer
Walk on them.

AGING

My mother teaches me something new every day
About aging, growing older,
Limitations, strength,
Determination, and
Wide-eyed knowing.

HEADACHE

When in the presence of those who do not support you,
Those who would rather see you fail than aid you
In any possible way,
When you know and they know that
Your way is the best, most effective,
Way of proceeding, but it is passed over,
Rejected and deemed non-applicable; and then
You see your project announced and slated for implementation,
A year later
And you rush to attend the meeting in
Which the project is announced
By and in the name of
The person who led the charge
Against you
In this case,
You may find yourself with
A headache.

OBSERVANT AND FOCUSED (RECOGNIZING AGGRESSION)

Stage one – the push
Using language to incite anger and strife
Stage two – the stab

POEMS, MAXIMS & EXTENDED THOUGHTS

False accusations
Stage three – antagonism
Seemingly well-meaning interlopers
Console and push harder:
"I wouldn't let her talk to me like that"
Stage four – the physical bump
"Oops, excuse me, I
Ran into you
By accident"
Stage 5 – self-preservation
Contact the
Equal Employment Opportunity Commission
Stage 6 – Retaliation
Contact the
Labor Board, and
Apply elsewhere, as you have come full-circle.

THE WIDENING OF THE GAP IN EDUCATIONAL ACHIEVEMENT

When in 1994 or so
Black children were labeled "At Risk"
There were no clear definitions beyond skin color
And neighborhood.

We have since learned
What they were at risk for:
Racism
Discrimination
Prejudice
Marginalization
Countertransference
Projection
Under-education
No education
Crime
Incarceration;
Free labor for corporate moguls.

HOLDING ONTO HATE

The human mechanism is incredibly capable of so many things;
We evolve from a single cell,
We grow inside of another human being,
We evolve from cell to zygote, to embryo, to fetus,
Human infant, and then

We are born
We learn to identify objects
We develop a sense of self
We recognized sights and sounds
We learn to communicate, even in the absence of sight or sound
We learn to walk
We do not always crawl first
We explore our world in the home
Where we are the brightest, best, and most loved.

We learn to talk and we are spoken to, read to
We learn the letters that gather together to make sounds,
That express sentiments
The knowledge we acquire prepares us
For the world outside of home.

When we enter school nearly everything we know can fall apart
Not everyone is welcoming
Not everyone likes the sound or shape of our name
Not everyone likes the way we look
The way we talk or the clothes and shoes we wear, or
The texture of our hair.

We learn that we are different
Because those with whom we enter the environment have been taught
To look out for us,
To be wary of us
To stay away from us
To come in close proximity, only
To taunt and tease us.

POEMS, MAXIMS & EXTENDED THOUGHTS

They have been taught to hate what they see, and to know
That they should hate us,
And to hold onto the hate for a lifetime.

NEW MATERIAL

No school for me for many years,
And I am sitting here among young, bright,
Eager to learn students, trying to
Convince myself that I can compete.
But wait, the professor is asking a question, and
Without warning my hand goes up all by itself!
I must know the answer.

FROM NARRATIVE TO FORMAL WRITING

From an early age, we can all tell a story from
Beginning, to middle, to end
And later, we can, if trained
And then prompted to do so,
Identify the rising and falling action of a performance, and the
Accompanying elements leading to resolution,

But when moving from narrative
To the scrutiny and evaluation
Of the writings of others.
We are met with difficulty . . . initially.

Formal writing demands that we develop the skills required
To read, identify argument,
Evaluate, and conclude something,
The real task is set before us;
We cannot just say whether we like the writing or not,

We have to identify the author's argument, which may be
Clearly stated or at best implied.
We have to understand the organization of writing,
We have to grasp how it unfolds and why.
We have to conclude something, and then

We have to write our own thesis/argument/claim
We have to use parts of the readings to support
Our interpretations, our perceptions,
We have to use and document sources.

We progress from narrative
To the world of discourse.
Complete with in-text citations, Works Cited pages, or
References pages, and annotated bibliographies.
The possibilities for our future
Are endless once we arrive at
This threshold of knowledge.

AGENDA

How can you accuse me of having an agenda
When I am Black and choose Black writers?
When I am Asian and choose Asian writers?
When I am Iranian and choose Iranian writers?
When I am Native American Indian and choose Native American Indian
    Writers?
When I am Spanish and choose only Spanish writers?
When I am Mexican and choose only Mexican writers?
When I am Jewish and choose Jewish writers?
When I am not White and choose anything that is not White
To teach?
What am I doing?
If I choose only White writers, I know that
I am diminishing the importance, quality, spirit, usefulness, and richness
Of other writers
Of other cultures.

STOLEN

Did you know that young girls
Aged twelve years and younger
Are missing in Alameda County USA, and other
Counties as well?

Children spirited away from malls,
Lured away from safe,
Loving homes (sometimes willingly),
Willingly escaping into the night
To be preyed upon by
Drug dealers, hustlers, and pimps
And the men and women who purchase them.
Did you know that there are agencies
And non-profit organizations
In place to *help*?
Agencies that systematically,
Lose the children in their custody?
The question then becomes:
If we know who the culprits are,
If we know who purchases the children for sex,
If we can set up sting operations to
Recover and return these children
To their families,
Then why does child trafficking still exist?
I suppose we could ask the same questions about
Prostitution, Drug trafficking, Human trafficking, Gun trafficking
And yet, here we are wondering what to do next.

SPIRITED AWAY

I don't want to be restricted in any way
I want to be free to roam, to hang out
There is something that I need,
Something that I am not getting here,
At home.

You don't see it, but I do.
You treat my sister better than me.
You look at her with loving eyes,
But not me.
You always say now pretty she is
While combing her long, wavy hair.
But you fuss and frown as you wrestle
With my kinky, thick brown hair

Someone out there is telling me that
I am beautiful.
He promises me beautiful things
And freedom.
When I sneak out at night to see him
He holds me close,
He strokes my cheek,
He looks into my eyes,
He loves me.

I am leaving . . .
Tonight.

COMING FROM ANOTHER PLACE

In my country, we do not talk like you do.
We do not write with these strange figures.
Words do not connote the same ideas.
I hear the words, but struggle to comprehend,
Struggle to write.
I know that it is important, learning this language called
English, but it is not easy for me.
So be patient, and I will try my best.
Be patient, and I will rise to the occasion.
Be patient because if I were writing in my own
Native language, every word, every concept
Would be perfectly written and articulated,
And you would be the one who does not understand.

WHERE DOES HATE COME FROM?

Hate and love come from a place where children are first indoctrinated,
    home.
Do parents and siblings unwittingly or intentionally teach hate through
Conversations, comments while watching movies or television, words spo-
ken during heated arguments, stereotyping, exhibited negative behaviors
towards new friends, and repeating seemingly harmless jokes?

Certainly some parents and siblings teach love by showing respect,
Discussing the damaging aspects of movies, sitcoms,
Or reality television shows that denigrate races of people and
Create new, unpalatable stereotypes.

Before children enter the socializing arena of public school
Communication-based activities in the home contribute widely to
Their perceptions of self and others,
And their ultimate placement in the world –

But be forewarned of kindergarten boot camp
Where the teacher first stands at the front of the classroom,
Deciding where students will sit,
With the power to segregate the classroom,
One row at a time, and establishing learning groups
The crows, the clowns, the eagles

Children trained to see differences, to know
The signs and engage in or be abused by racism and discrimination,
Even at five-years old, can answer with detail the question:
Did anything happen at school today that made you feel uncomfortable?

INTO THE NIGHT AND LOST FOREVER
(AN INTERIOR MONOLOGUE)

I remember thinking, "I can't stay here anymore
I only missed one class and I'm grounded. Give me a break!
Well, I won't take this. Let's see, it's midnight, I'm out!

Wow, it's really dark out here.
Things look different.
I'll just ride the train to the end of the line,
Wherever that is.
Here comes the bus.

These people look really strange.
The ride to the train station never seemed this long.
I'll show my parents. They'll be sorry that they

Grounded me. There's a familiar face. I saw him on campus today as I was
    leaving."
"Hey, mind if I sit next to you? Where to?" he said.

All of this happened a year ago, and now I don't know how to get back
    home;
I don't even know where I am.

JUST GET A JOB

Getting a job is not that simple.
Not only does one have to be qualified,
One also has to "fit." And yet, this word
Is never mentioned in a job description.
"Fit" supersedes knowledge, education, and
Work experience.

"Fit" happens when one is finally *visual*,
Can be seen, sitting in front
Of the hiring principles.

Whether one fits into the
Scheme of things can be discerned at this time: it
Eliminates the possibility that one can be hired
Based on meeting all qualifications.

IDLE MIND

An idle mind can't wait
To fill an atmosphere with turmoil.
It is in complete control.
It knows that in the throes of anger, you will blow.
It relies on the vulnerability of the body.

An idle mind needs you.
After all, it cannot operate alone and
Has nothing else to do
Except direct you.

POEMS, MAXIMS & EXTENDED THOUGHTS

A mind that is cluttered
Promotes the same type of blank stare,
As it seeks to unravel the structured lives of others,
So friends fall away and you are left alone.
A mind that is cluttered embraces madness.
Its sense of self engulfs you in sadness,
And your mind becomes destructive.

CONFLICT IN CONSCIOUSNESS

This strange thing
Happens to you,
A conflict in consciousness.
When met with a choice
To be the person whom one is
Inside, or
To be the person whom one is
Expected to be
Outside.
You don't get it?

Okay, I mean,
We have been friends
Since childhood,
Sleepovers,
Camping trips,
Birthday parties,
Best friends for life, and

When we got here,
Arrived on
This college campus,
Separated by sororities,
Dorms,
Acceptance and
Denial,
Respectfully,
You changed, but

When we go home,
Like now,
For spring break, or
Summer break, or
Christmas, or
Easter . . .
You show up at my
House, warm, loving
Wanting to
Spend time
With me
Thinking we
Are friends
Again.
Guess What? We are not.

WAS IT REALLY LIKE THAT?

I learned that Black people,
African people,
Were ripped from their homes,
Their sacred lands,
In Africa
And forced onto ships,
Slave ships, and
Into small, cramped spaces
In the bellies of those ships
Packed side-by-side,
Beneath, and on top of one another.
Reading it made me so sad
That I cried,
But there was more.

When they came up for air,
Those who survived,
Being vomited on,
Defecated on,
Urinated on, and more
Were whipped,

Beaten for no reason,
No reason at all,
Except,
That they were Black,
African, enslaved.
Learning all of this
Made me cry even harder,
But there was more.

Sometimes, while standing on deck
When no one was
Looking,
Men, Women and their babies,
Disappeared into the sea,
Purposely choosing
Death over an unknown life.
I cried and cried,
But there was more.

Those who arrived on
Distant shores
With their families in tact
Were separated,
Sold like cattle,
Like slabs of meat,
Auctioned off like
Antique furniture,
To the highest bidder.
Mothers were separated
From their Infants,
Husbands were separated from their wives,
The tight unyielding hands of
Brothers and sisters
Yanked apart.
These losses did not impact
The onlookers.
I cried ever harder.

I wondered,
"How could people actually live through stuff like that.

How could people be so cruel? What kind of
People condemn, dehumanize, and seek
To control others for financial gain?"
And then I stopped reading, turned on the
News, and saw a Black man shot and killed
Right before my eyes.
I saw every aspect of the shooting
It was as if I were standing there,
A witness
Thanks to live, cell phone reporting,
I was stunned
But there was more . . . the officer was acquitted.

FOR YOU, GRANDDAUGHTER

To the one who has risen from
Inquisitive, crawling infant to
Stunningly, beautiful, intelligent
Woman.
The one who listens attentively,
And loves with open arms.
The one who learned all over again
To know and trust that our love
Was, is, and will always be real.
Congratulations on all that you have
And will, accomplish.

CUTTING (FOR CASEY)

Sometimes cutting means
Carving oneself
Into
Existence.

"AHHHHHHHHHH . . . "

I can breathe,
I am free,
I will survive.

Photo ©2016 Akil Foster

THE KIEN EVOLUTION

Pugs at Gramma's house
Te-Te and Tony
Bubbles and Elmo.
Ballet, "Is that Kien?"
"Yeah, she's the cat."
Calico Critters®
4-pack play set
Koala bears, brown bears
No rabbits, please
Trip to Japan
Othello *is* about racism!
Fruits Basket®
Everything Anime
Copic® sketch markers,

These colors only, please.
Cell phone and new pajamas
Off to Japan, again
Lap top computer, please
Cap and gown
Off to New York . . . to be continued

MOM, GRANDMOTHER, GREAT-GRANDMOTHER: THINGS I, WE DID NOT SAY

Many years ago, you stopped
Hugging me, all of us.
We cannot be sure right now,
But that will probably be one of the things
That we will miss,
Most of all, about you;
The hugs, the reassurance of your love.
But, maybe it was not you
Who did all of the hugging,
Maybe it was me, all of us
Who hugged you first,
And you who hugged back.
Maybe it was me, all of us
Who stopped hugging you.
So before we have to acknowledge
That we miss those hugs.
We, all of us, will start
Hugging you
Every chance we get.

Exercise

2

EXERCISE WORKSHEET FOR SMALL GROUP DISCUSSION AND SECOND WRITING ASSIGNMENT

PART I: Using a library database or search engine, find related articles prompted by the reading of one or two maxims (child-trafficking, cutting, microaggressions, discrimination, etc.). List the poems and articles on the worksheet, and make note of your findings - the ways that your understanding is broadened by additional information derived from research (use additional paper if needed).

1.

2.

PART II: Select one maxim to rewrite in your own words.

Homework Assignment:
Write an essay that speaks to what you learned after researching a selected topic prompted by one or two maxims. <u>A complete description of this assignment will be distributed in class.</u> Modern Language Association (MLA) style is required. Remember to include your rewrite of an existing maxim. Use your handbook!

Attach this worksheet to your completed assignment.

Exercise   3

SELF-PORTRAIT

PART III: Find a picture or portrait of yourself as a child. Attach it to this worksheet and think about who you were then. Jot down notes that come into your consciousness.

Next, create a poem or short story about . . . *The Person in the Picture.* Answer the following questions:
1. Who were you then?
2. What was your day-to-day existence like? Describe it.
3. What elements of that person remain with you today?
4. How have you changed?

Place your notes here, and attach this worksheet to your written assignment.

Extended Thoughts

3

Photo ©2016 Akil Foster

SALAMANDERS

Young people have unique ways of falling into traps; like salamanders, they walk to the edge and fall off. They are not born with wings and the ability to fly over the peaks and valleys of life that wait to consume them. They cannot soar over the edge to safety. Paraphrasing Nikki Giovanni, it is our responsibility to teach the young to fly. Young people will get what they need to survive in their process of development. They will ask for it, or they will take it. Parents are responsible for a child's security, growth, education, development, perception of love and respect, and his or her spiritual connection. Parents are empowered to teach a child what love means, and they can also fill the child's mind with strategically directed hate.

When the magic age arrives, usually age twelve, and brings on the phase that can easily be called the "understanding zero" syndrome, difficult times loom ominously ahead, waiting in the passageways of the mind, affecting both children and parents. A child's "absorbent mind," borrowing a phrase from Maria Montessori, develops into a selective, discriminating mass of knowledge and impressions quite capable of making choices that are not always good ones. Puberty marks the "Rite of Passage" stage through which some of our children pass and some do not survive. Schools, churches, community-based organizations, brothers and sisters, grandparents, mothers and fathers, directors, producers, drug dealers, pimps, and the news media all contribute to the information disseminated to these impressionable minds. Who will win? Who will take control and lead the child?

School systems have more rules and guidelines governing disciplinary action than there are rules and guidelines related to teacher-conduct in the classroom. Many teachers, I suspect, are in position to ensure that a large percentage of children of color, particularly Black males, fail. It is most difficult to believe that these teachers do not intentionally set out on this path.

There is a climate of hate brewing in the classrooms of many elementary, primary, and secondary public schools. The students are the victims. Parents and youth must acknowledge their share of responsibility, but the often negative behavior in the classroom coming from educators themselves takes a toll on unsuspecting students, and yet the students are often blamed and subsequently punished. Time is spent in assessing the students' behaviors, and little or none is spent assessing exactly what goes on in the classroom, behind the door. Children are driven from the classroom, out of the mainstream, and into detention halls, counselors' offices, and continuation schools where dedicated teachers try to repair the damage, or not.

Rules are good to have, we all need rules of conduct, but if these rules only apply to a selected few, then a conclusion can be draws that a separation process is in place and working to alienate students, to drive them purposely away from education. Where do they go? They go into the streets, into juvenile systems, and then into privatized prison systems, jails. Parents, wealthy and poor, wonder what is happening to the children. The answer may be that their spirits are empty and that they lack the inner drive to save themselves.

Teachers know their power. Some of them wield it in favor of the students, and some of them use it to manipulate, frustrate, and coerce students into the trap of negative behavior, and then kick them out. If teachers take a symbolic foot and kick our students in the head, daily, then what can be expected but students who seize the opportunity to strike back? In striking back, the students almost certainly seal their own fates since no one seems to be on their side. So they fall off the edge and plunge into the valley of uncertainty and self-destruction.

Brothers and sisters are, for some youth, the only role models available. The younger children are always watching, learning, and absorbing. If the model is positive, children will learn to be leaders; if the model is negative, children may become followers, unable to make sense of life, unable to establish reasons for existing, and unable to make decisions on their own. All adults will acknowledge that mistakes are made throughout the life cycle, but current times carry heavier consequences; prison cells are polished and waiting to consume a new generation of inmates – new prison beds are waiting to be filled. Pay attention to the signs: If less money is going into prevention (i.e., after-school programs, intramural sports options, community-based programs, internship programs, and summer youth employment programs), and more money is being secured to build jails . . . something is terribly wrong.

Grandparents of yesterday are scarce; the grandparents of today are often forced into parenting by the shadow of death, the destruction of drugs, and the power of a locked jail cell. On the other hand, some grandparents are too young, too busy, and overwhelmed by their own struggles: trying to find jobs to support the family, trying to find suitable living conditions, trying to deal with the school systems, and trying to survive. These difficulties make it nearly impossible to see clearly the needs of their grandchildren. There is a great deal of difference between ruling with love as an extension of peace of mind, and ruling with the fist or strap, owing to the frustration and anger that trickles down after a single day of disappointment and defeat.

The television is not kind. It does not care who watches it; it responds with a variety of programs when turned on. If it serves as a babysitter, it may teach lessons children are not prepared to learn. Although good educational programming is available, not many children, left alone, will select appropriate channels. Video games teach manual dexterity and creativity, but can also teach the joy of killing, seeking revenge, and destroying property. With the latest technology becoming accessible to a wider audience, social media has opened the door to bullies and other unsavory characters. In a hypnotic state, communicating with players globally, children hold their controllers and kill, or sever someone's head, and then cheer at their victories. The screen before them is bloody. On the other hand, think about it, if the desire is to become a graphic artist or designer of video grams, learning how to create images and program them to move in and out of corridors, or to animate figures so that they can be blown up with blood flowing as a fantasy, that is one thing, but if what is being implanted in the mind is something more sinister, then there is a problem. Children need help in understanding strange messages. They need to be made aware of the mental process of separating reality from imagination. When a screenwriter intends to juxtapose the negative with the positive, children often miss the message and get caught up in the violence; they may choose their heroes by the size and scope of their weapons.

Drug dealers are way ahead of state and local government officials, law enforcement, the family, the church, and advocates for children. They already understand that the children have great potential to lead and to make money, so the children are manipulated by the power of money. When children perceive themselves as having nothing and cannot foresee ever possessing anything of value, including their own lives, they can become easy prey for drug dealers or pimps and lose all connection with family, education, and a viable future. For many children, tomorrow is not expected to come. They feel compelled to get all they can, as fast as they can. If they are young enough, they can establish their reputations on the street as "hard." They can live the "life" until one of their "brothers" shoots and kills them, or until the police capture or trap them, or until they overdose on drugs, or until they *commit suicide* in their cells.

People of Color in America's society are trying to survive, trying to believe, trying to exist. What message is being sent to the children? Look into some of the faces of our youth; they are capable of doing great things. If allowed to develop and grow their names will appear on honor rolls, they will be accepted at major universities and other four-year institutions, they will be busy finding cures for AIDS, cancer, and other life threatening diseases. Hold fast to the possibility of all children thriving, growing,

POEMS, MAXIMS & EXTENDED THOUGHTS

and learning in the classroom mainstream, instead of being relegated to remedial reading courses and continuation schools. Imagine children engaged and working hard in the direction of productive futures for themselves and their own children. Children forced to persevere in a world that closes doors, can adapt and gain powerful inner strength, strength that will enable those precious salamanders to adapt, stop and turn away from the edge, to metamorphose into eagles with the ability to soar and reach heights that at first seemed impossible. We can and must teach our children to hold onto life and to stop killing each other in the streets. Without children, a future is impossible.

Photo ©2016 Akil Foster

PEOPLE OF COLOR

"While on the path of life, if you come across some strange overgrown insect sitting on a leaf smoking an obnoxious pipe, don't ask him which way you should go . . . take out your compass." (Chriss Foster)

People of Color have been so well deprived of truth in history that its revelation causes immediate anger and frustration. For example, in 1945, bus companies in the state of Alabama were ordered to enforce segregation, so when in 1955, Mrs. Rosa Parks chose to ride while sitting in the front of the bus, she made the choice because she was "tired of giving in." That simple act, which resulted in her arrest, carried deeply felt messages throughout the world that Black people were excluded from sitting where they pleased on public transportation; they could not eat or drink where White people chose to eat and drink; and, they could not expect to become gainfully employed. Why was it ever a problem in the first place? Why was and is America so unwilling to extend equal rights to all people? It is now 2016, and the "Bus Ride" is still not over.

Black people are still punished for daring to achieve, to strive for equality in primary, secondary and post-secondary institutions, as well as positions in the structure of corporate America. We are punished for insisting that we are part of the "We The People " connection and that we have rights, and we want our true history included in text books not as an aside, but as an integral part of the building blocks of education. What was our crime? Some of our ancestors were wrenched from the Motherland, Africa, bought and sold like cattle in America; forced to give up families, children, and spouses. In protest, on the journey to America, some of our ancestors jumped to their deaths overboard distraught from their losses, and unwilling to come here. But some Black people came willingly as indentured servants and acquired levels of wealth on their own plantations. When Black people dared to stand up for themselves, they were shot or hanged and became the "Strange Fruit" hanging from southern trees that Billy Holiday sang about, or the lifeless figures in jail cells at the end of a rope, or in today's world, a plastic bag. We worked in the fields and cultivated the soil to feed the world. We were kindly given the entrails of pigs to prepare for our meals, and expected to appreciate the gesture; we were not allowed to read if we were able to, and certainly not allowed to learn to read if we could not, and even our family names were changed. We were stripped of everything and forced to serve, fight, and die. But we are not the only ones who suffered.

Among the many atrocities perpetrated against them, the Chinese struggled to build the railways in the Nevada Mountains, during winter months of heavy snow. Many lost their lives in avalanches, and nobody bothered to recover their bodies until spring. Native American Indians were slaughtered and stripped of their land. The Japanese brought thriving businesses to America, only to have their businesses wrenched away during World War II, as they were relegated to concentration camps. And, there was a time when Mexican Americans, whose original land is now American soil complete with borders designed to keep them out of it, were brave enough to fight for America, but they were not permitted burial alongside White soldiers. We are all still fighting to survive. And what did we manage to become as a result of our endless battles?

We are doctors, researchers, nuclear physicists, neonatologists, lawyers, judges, educators, engineers, property owners, managers, supervisors, married with children, Presidents, First ladies, and First families of the Unites States of America. We are role models for generations to come, and still we are referred to with labels: low socioeconomic status, minorities, "At Risk," the "N" word, and we have to struggle and sometimes fight to be included. Opportunities are diminishing; drugs and disease continue to infiltrate our communities on a grand scale, and we have turned against each other.

When Affirmative Action opened the door for one or two positions for "already-more-than-qualified" than anyone else *People of Color* to enter universities, lawsuits attacked universities claiming reverse discrimination. But no one commented on the discrimination part that which kept Black students at an enrollment level between 1% - 3% before and after Affirmative Action, and yet even in the face of this adversity, some of us dared to succeed anyway. However, it is apparent that some measures must be taken to stop the rest of us. But we need not buy into the plan by feeding the process. A negative climate is growing. We are divided by our own critical, non-productive, non-supportive behavior, coupled with the cards that are stacked against us. Our pain and strife run so deep that the frustration emerges in self-destructive behavior. Unity, for the most part, is lost so that the "village" required to raise the children no longer exists. Some of us barely survive as shadows of lost souls with double-edged destinies. And in this broken state, which includes a male versus female dynamic, we are still held responsible for the world's most invaluable assets, the children.

FINDING A SENSE OF PURPOSE

I entered the college classroom as a teacher to inspire students to read, to write, and to express themselves. Most importantly, I wanted to ensure that students learned to seek the value in the prize, the prize being knowledge. I was scared, and my new students were too. Adjusting to college curriculum is difficult after being away from the classroom for many years. It is also difficult when no foundation is laid beforehand, and it is particularly upsetting when students become the end result of poor education. During that first year, as I met and watched the development of a variety of students, a wonderful thing happened: *I began to learn,* and I discovered the depth of responsibility the title "teacher" carries. I believe the desire to learn and grow academically exists within everyone. A teacher's purpose is to help students discover where their desires are hidden. The teacher must dig them out, dust them off, and then help students to fulfill them. I see, in some students' faces, expressions of frustration, doubt, and self-defeat. I remember feeling the same emotions during my first semester at the University of California at Berkeley. So I always share it with them.

I remember wondering who Virginia Woolf was and what she could possibly have to teach me through her collection of novels. A reading assignment introduced me to the short essay titled "Kew Gardens." Virginia Woolf's description of this magnificent place, the people who passed through it, and the life issues they endured taught me how to visualize the world from different perspectives, to see that even the life of a single snail mattered, as it traversed the earth beneath the visitors at Kew gardens. Her use of descriptive language enabled me to get close enough to see the blue veins on the snail's back that carried its life's blood and assured its existence just like the veins that allowed the blood to flow through the bodies of the people who walked past it, people who had goals and objectives, moving through life just like the seemingly insignificant snail. In other Woolf novels, I followed the stream-of-consciousness narrative of *Mrs. Dalloway* through frustrations that in the end granted her the peace found in her tears and silent thoughts. I moved in and out with *The Waves* depicting the symbolic ebb and flow of lives from early childhood through and including death. I experienced the angst of a little boy anticipating a long awaited journey *To The Lighthouse* and discovered the impact of a broken promise on child and wife. As reading captured me in a new and exciting way, I saw the fatal wolf-like image of Prosper Merimee's *Carmen*, and understood the difficulty of womanhood that pits courage, honor, and cultural expectations against the possibility of love and lasting relationships. I pitied Giuseppe Verdi's *Rigoletto*, a man who lost his daughter and his dignity, caught up in the duality of character, the doubling that forbids one the opportunity to view oneself in the all important mirror of life, a man whose social status and love for his daughter could not alter the position of the noble and privileged Duke; an all too familiar positioning of the super rich having power over the poor. So difficult was the first reading of Kafka's *The Metamorphosis*, trying to understand his connection to the antagonist Gregor Samsa, and finally recognizing the desire to tuck oneself neatly away inside when life becomes too much to bear. Intrigued, I marveled at the "sentences" written in human blood, and imagined the needles of the harrow piercing and tearing human flesh *In the Penal Colony*, and recognized the struggle, the intense fight for individuality and completeness, the need for acceptance, acceptance denied and viewed as a crime against society. And then I embarked on the forbidden path in *The Castle*, which led to an unbearable reality, a place where the minds of men and women were altered, rendering automatons addicted to a strange substance. I came to understand Kafka through the desire and hunger of *A Hunger Artist* who sought recognition for his talent, just as Kafka sought recognition from his father for trying to be a good, obedient son. Many years later, I discovered the novels of Toni Morrison—*The Bluest Eye, Song of Solomon, Beloved, A Mercy, Home, Desdemona, God Bless The Child, and others*; and Alice Walker—*By the Light of My Father's Smile, In Search of Our Mothers' Gardens, Possessing the Secret Joy, Warrior Marks, The Color Purple, Living By The Word, We are the Ones We Have Been Waiting For: Inner Light in a Time of Darkness*, and more—these authors and their writings and many more shaped me as an educator—stories about life, expectations, resistance, and power; every novel, every story, every word—the most powerful writings that I have experienced to date. These novels represent only a handful of examples of the excellent writing that I think every student at some point should read no matter what his or her major is. After reading and studying the words of these and other great writers, I began to understand that writers are especially talented people who dare to write, who dare to express themselves in print for the world to experience. The written word is a powerful tool that can last forever if carefully embraced, protected, and passed on.

Students cannot expect that everything they are required to read will be of interest to them, but they can be carefully persuaded if educators are readers themselves and can present those titles that will engage and encourage students to read more and often. This means that the experience of teaching must encourage teachers to grow and continually expand their knowledge bases. Teaching can become the bridge that closes cultural gaps where understanding and acceptance are lacking. Students entering the classroom with open minds should be met with teachers who welcome freedom of expression and critical thinking. Reading literature is to explore every corner of the world's development. Literature incorporates life and history through the words of authors. Literature is an expression of time and place, of personal experiences, of historical events and impressions.

POEMS, MAXIMS & EXTENDED THOUGHTS

EUCALYPTUS LEAVES

Eucalyptus leaves, gathered in the early morning sun, soil the hands with a dusty black oil and a powerful scent that penetrates the senses.

This morning the sun shines bright and warms my body. I wonder if there will be snakes beneath fallen branches. Hot, so hot the day promises to be. As I tug at the branches, preparing the eucalyptus leaves, breaking leaves from safety within the shadow of each branch, something tugs at me; it is fear.

Hours roll by slowly at first, and then quickly as the sun threatens to rise too soon and force my journey to begin. I am destined to be off, up a strange road, climbing mountains and trails, leading to unknown ends, a new experience. I soothe and terrorize myself for hours, hoping that something, anything will come up and put this adventure off yet another day, another week, another month, forever. But the time is now. So, as always, I pretend to be brave, not wanting to disappoint anyone, not wanting to hear, "I told you she wasn't going." I hate having to admit I am afraid; I have formed the habit of making excuses, but not this time.

On the road, cities pass by unfamiliar, as if I have never seen them before, but I have traveled this road many times. Somewhere near San Jose, I see a clearing that stands still. It is green and brown, muddy and wet. I nervously chuckle at the thought that at any moment a dinosaur will appear; I just know it. I watch even as we pass it by until I feel the pain in my neck and carefully turn forward again. I think that I am the dinosaur emerging after years of stillness, years of burial beneath the weight of work, work, and more work. I sigh deeply and ride in silence.

Suddenly, the truck ascends, climbing to elevations above sea level. The curves ahead are overwhelming, weaving in and out under the wheels of a truck driving far too fast for my comfort. I close my eyes and pray as if I can amass the power to prevent the truck from going over the edge. My stomach knots up. This is a familiar feeling, a feeling that lets me know that I am taking a risk. I am so terrified now that I take mental leave.

In my mind I revisit all the places where I met fear previously; there is a long list: the dead-end rooms of *The Winchester House*; a drop-off point in the middle of Lake Berryessa; the slide at the Fun House in San Francisco; the roller coaster at *The Boardwalk* in Santa Cruz, the first flight, a car accident, an allergic reaction to habanero peppers, and more. I stop the mental review just short of an anxiety attack. I feel the truck slowing down and return to the present. I open my eyes and see a landscape that is incredibly beautiful. I acknowledge that had I not come, I would not have had this opportunity to *see*. I would have missed this serenity, this quiet, and this beauty.

The truck stops near the Ranger Station. I get out and run to the restroom. On the way back, I stop in the gift shop and remember that I want to buy a walking stick for my father. I promise myself that I will purchase it before we begin the ride back home. This promise is meant to indirectly inform God that I really want to return safely so that I can purchase a gift for my father, and that I hope he or she will afford me that opportunity.

The hike begins. One step in front of the other brings me closer to my fear because it is all so unfamiliar; I do not know what to expect, and I do not know where the trail will take me. I walk and begin to find a sense of peace. As the trail begins to elevate, I feel the challenge presented to my body, mind, and spirit. I nearly defeat myself at the outset. I do not want to be here, but I have come, so I have to go through with it. Each time I look up to see where I am going, my legs weaken and my spirit falters. I keep going.

Higher and higher I climb and, just when I think I will surely throw myself over the edge and end the torture, four little old ladies appear out of nowhere. Are they real or are they apparitions? They are wearing bright shirts, straw hats, and walking shoes. They have walking sticks too, like the one I will buy for my father. They appear robust, strong and smiling. One carries a branch of eucalyptus leaves. In single file, they trudge along past me and say, "We'll see you at the river." As they pass, my energy quickens. I feel stronger. Onward and upward, the trail winds in and out of mountains. I stand on the edge of a cliff and look up, not down. I am terrified, and I am in the wilderness of my soul.

Four hours later, on a sheer cliff, I feel compelled to look down. I see, for the first time, the tops of redwood trees. I am hypnotized for a moment by the beauty, power of nature, and the power of God so much so that I am nearly drawn over the edge, and this terrifies me even more. But I pull myself together because there is no other choice. I wonder why I am here and why I have not yet fallen off the edge. At this moment I can neither go forward, nor can I retreat. I just stand here, paralyzed. I realize my predicament and some inner force allows me to continue.

The trail continues up, around and through. I wonder when a snake, or rat, or mountain lion for that matter, will jump out and cause me to plummet over the edge, but nothing happens. My imagination is working overtime. I keep walking. The sound of running water pierces an eerie silence. I walk faster because the incline has flattened out, temporarily, and the faster I walk, the clearer the sound of water becomes. Now I stand in the stream. The water is flowing from the rocks somewhere above. It is clear and fresh. I drink slowly after collecting the water and pouring it through a filter—I feel refreshed. I think of home and force the fear that something will go wrong and I will never return way down inside. I begin to feel safe. I cannot seem to make a connection. I fill my water bottle again and keep going.

The sun beats down upon me in the dry spots, so I rest. I am not aware that the place where I rest is where the rattlesnakes reside, the place where my legs demand that I stop. The shade cools and soothes me between the mountains, where the mosquitoes wait for the blood of life, my blood. Periodically, I replenish the thick coating of insect repellent on my face, arms, and legs. I climb over and under fallen trees. I leap across ravines that wait for me to lose my footing so that they can engulf me and hide my body from rescuers. I step aside on a narrow road for hikers on their way down and wish I was going with them. I smile a nervous smile as hikers pass me by. I encourage my feet, with silent words, to lift and fall on command. By now, I am exhausted, scared, and determined. I cannot fall behind.

Finally, the trail is beginning to decline. I run like a naked two-year-old after a bath. I feel the wind on my face and relief in my legs. I feel free and strong. Down, down, down I run. At the bottom I see a beautiful river. It is clear and cold. I shiver as if I am touching an electrical current. I attempt to walk the rocks, but find myself ankle deep in cold water. I gasp. Once on the other side, I look for the little old ladies, but convinced that they were not real, I shrug, and seek a new adventure. I walk on, loving the flatness of the earth but cursing the troublesome rocks. I am happy knowing that I have arrived safely, so I whisper a prayer to God and once again mention the walking stick the I want to purchase, reiterating *our* deal.

As I help to clear the cluttered earth for the patiently waiting tent, fear once again seizes me. I know I will have to hike back out in a few days. I push the unruly fear way deep down inside and prepare to rest. I cook and eat food over a campfire. Imagine that! I learn to respect my surroundings. I bathe and am baptized in the river. I sit naked and vulnerable in the mineral baths while exploring the artwork of mineral deposits. I rest; I am at peace with myself.

Night is falling. I need to sleep. I trust my faith to keep me from harm. The solid earth accepts the sleeping bag and the weight of my body graciously. The moonlight enters and illuminates the cavern of the tent within which I sleep. The music I hear comes from chirping crickets. I drop off to sleep and my vision incorporates the power of my imagination once again. I see mountain lions, bears, snakes, and then fish swimming silently in the river. I am forced awake by the pressure of something on my legs and feet. Terror grips me as I prepare to die; then I relax as I see and acknowledge that two large protective Rottweilers having protected me on the trail found comfort sleeping across my body to guard and protect me while I slept. I settle in and sleep soundly. My body heat soothes me. I am safe.

Morning comes too soon. No clock signals the time for night eyes to receive daylight. No rooster crows. The sun warms the earth and speaks loudly of the time for rising. The river is here to greet me with fresh, cold, soothing water. Oatmeal and raisins never tasted this good. Carrots and broccoli nourish me. Canned fish provide a meal fit for any Black King, Queen, or child of nobility. I know that this peacefulness cannot last.

POEMS, MAXIMS & EXTENDED THOUGHTS

I sit in the mineral bath on the evening of the fourth day. In the morning it will be time to go, time to climb back up and then down to civilization. Back to Civilization? On the contrary, I will be leaving civilization and returning to the rush of life, the urgency to achieve, to compete, to struggle. My feet feel numb; the fear is returning. My throat is dry. My body is trembling. My mind is working hard to convince me that I cannot make it. I will not listen this time.

Back on the trail, I allow myself to look down and over the edge of the cliff. I see the greenery. I am in awe of the majesty of nature in its state of being. Did I pass this way before? Yes, but my fear kept me from seeing and appreciating the full scope of beauty. I move quickly at times, slowly when tired, and renewed when the trail levels out. I watch for poison oak and ivy. I watch, again, for snakes and other creatures upon whose turf I am treading. I wait for that familiar feeling. Fear does not arise in me.

There is only one mile left to walk. A snake, an infant at best, appears and disappears. It does not allow me the time to get all worked up. I smile and walk on. Around the bend, seated securely and facing out over the cliff, I see two llamas and a huge mastiff. They are all golden wheat in color and blend into the rocks. I maneuver around them. To my surprise I see another llama ahead. This one is sitting broad across the trail. His back is turned toward me. I wonder how I will get around him. He is magnificent; his massive body is strong with a majestic presence. I fight the urge to kneel. He is Black; a kindred spirit. He sits with his body tall and regal as if he owns and is an extension of the trail; I am an intruder. I walk carefully up to him and stroke his coarse, black hair. He does not move his body, but turns his head in my direction. The look in his eyes acknowledges my uneasiness and accepts my presence. He shifts just a little and allows me to pass. He is chewing eucalyptus leaves.

Before long the trail widens. The park area is busy with people sounds. The hike is over, and I am filled with a special kind of joy. I go to the truck to retrieve my wallet, and then walk to the Ranger Station to purchase the walking stick for my father. On the ride home, I keep my eyes open and watch the winding cliffs disappear behind me, as the truck descends the high road. I feel a calming force. I breathe accomplishment. I leave my fear behind. I am grateful that God, The Creator, allowed me to live through this experience. I am stronger now. I think about the little old ladies, convinced that they never really existed. I believe they were spirits, a vision for my eyes only, and the river they spoke of is yet to come.

Eucalyptus leaves, gathered in the early morning sun, soil the hands with a dusty, black oil, and a powerful scent that penetrates the senses.

BENEATH IT ALL

The housekeeper came promptly three days during the week. I worked steadily on my computer, trying to complete yet another project. She was quiet and efficient, so little or no communication was necessary. I kept my pace and, as always, she came to me and said, "Miss?, there is something stuck under the sofa and I cannot get it out." I waved her away and said, "Don't worry about it, I'll get it out someday." This brief exchange had gone on for over a year.

The "something" she spoke of had been there long before she was employed. After a long, lonely winter I had discovered it in the garage connected to my house. After a move to the country, I hadn't bothered to explore the property, but had settled in and started to write. The sofa was not level, so I wandered around in the garage and retrieved the odd-shaped rock-like object; the "something" that had been placed in storage. I used it to balance the uneven legs of the sofa in the den where I wrote. I had always been careful to sweep around it because I soon discovered that once it settled into the floor, I could not move it, and its presence made it impossible to lift the heavy sofa after awhile. I tried pulling it out, but could not get a grip on it, so I just left it alone. One evening, sitting by the fireplace, I decided to give it one more try. I tried to lift the sofa, I tried to pull it out, and I tried to dig it out with a stick. After complete exhaustion set in, I gave up. It obviously belonged where it was.

Years passed, seasons changed, and people came into and disappeared out of my life. The cleaning lady continued to come and work silently and finally stopped asking about the "something" under the sofa. I forgot about it completely.

There comes a time in every life when one feels old and empty. This feeling had grown over the years. My children were grown and too selfish to have children of their own, so I was alone with my work and my pug, Adisa, most of the time, hearing from or seeing them only when they needed something. When my daughter finally announced that she was pregnant, I had a glimmer of hope. I had always vowed to be sailing on the Queen Elizabeth II, therefore, unavailable for babysitting, but I never really meant that I would not be delighted to have grandchildren.

And when Kristopher arrived, I had to cancel my mental cruise ticket. He was full of life and grew to question everything. He called me *Damma*. I taught him how to use my computer and read stories to him. I took him on short business trips to ensure that he would never fear flying. By the time he was four years old, he was carrying on major conversations with a philosophical air. We spent great weekends together. I especially liked the fact that he asked wonderful questions, and then sat quietly for answers. He would go away to think, and then return with an evaluation of the answer. As luck would have it, he discovered the "something" under the sofa.

I was busy working and listening to music one day while he was visiting. He, as always, wandered around the house, playing with Adisa, coming to check on my progress periodically. He had become accustomed to asking why I never smiled. I could not answer this question. I was thinking about that very thing as the sun went down. Suddenly I realized that I had not seen him for quite some time. A feeling of panic came over me. I felt strange and awkward. I thought I was having an anxiety attack.

Oddly enough, I could not move. Feeling something approaching, I turned around. There he stood with the "something" in his hands. It was huge in those tiny hands. Smiling, he said, "It's warm and it's moving." I wanted to take it from him, fearing that it would harm him in some way, but I could not lift my arms.

The "something" began to shed dust and dirt. It pulsated and glowed. I sat in horror, but Kristopher was not afraid. As the dust and dirt fell to the floor, my chest began to rise and fall; my lungs struggled to take in oxygen. Our eyes widened simultaneously and met as the "something" took shape. "Damma!" he shouted, "It's your heart." As he said the words it moved in a flash from his hands and disappeared into my chest. He ran to me and said, "Damma, you're smiling."

THE DEAD CAT

On a Monday morning during office hours, I peered out my office window and remarked to myself how clear and blue the sky was, and then I looked down. I saw what appeared to be a beautiful black cat. Its hair was rich and silky, and it seemed to be sleeping peacefully, curled into a neat ball.

On Friday of the same week, I opened and looked out the window. I looked down and saw the cat again, but suspected this time that it was not asleep, as it was in the exact same position and somewhat bloated. Thinking the worst, I called the business office and suggested that someone call the American Society for Prevention of Cruelty to Animals (ASPCA). I closed the window assured that someone would come and inspect the situation and remove the carcass of the cat. In fact, as I left the office three men were gathered around the cat beneath my window like the *Three Wine Tasters*, so I was certain that at least one of them would determine how to take care of the problem.[1]

On the following Monday, the weather was cold, so I did not open my window, and yet the cat was on my mind; however, I did not look. I just assumed that it was gone. But on Wednesday, When I opened my window and looked down, there on the ground was the infested carcass of the cat with wisps of hair scattered about. This scene brought about immediate

---

1. The "Vinegar Tasters," a Taoist painting, shows three great Chinese philosophers: Confucius, Buddha, and Lau Tzu, as they taste vinegar from a huge pot and show different reactions.

POEMS, MAXIMS & EXTENDED THOUGHTS

nausea. I called the business office, and demanded that someone please come to take care of the rotting carcass beneath my office window to which the same three men responded promptly, and again stood in a circle around the now rotting carcass under my window. Determined not to ever open my window again, I packed up my briefcase and left the office for the day.

Office hours for the next week were held without opening the window. The vision of the rotting carcass of the cat would not dissipate. Every time I entered the office, I thought about that cat, or what used to be the cat, half eaten by who knows what. A month after the last visit from business office and maintenance personnel, I decided that I could open my window without worrying about a dead animal beneath it. Surely, there would be no dead cat. So with trepidation, I approached the window and opened it, standing there for a full minute before looking down. There on the ground were the scattered bones and hints of black hair of what used to be a beautiful black cat. I have long since relocated my office.

Exercise 4

The previous readings: "Salamanders," "People of Color," "Finding a Sense of Purpose," "Eucalyptus Leaves," "Beneath It All," and "The Dead Cat" all represent the contemplation of real situations.

Part I: Annotate two readings of choice by writing in the margins and underlining passages for discussion. Brainstorm ways to bring a discussion of the readings to your peers. List three major questions:

1.

2.

3.

Part II: Select an additional reading, and write a comparison and contrast essay (additional instructions will be distributed in class). List your selections here, and write an extended list of key points (an outline) to be covered in your essay, and attach this form to your assignment.

Selection title I:

Selection title II:

Key points (for comparison and contrast):

EXPLORING THE WRITTEN WORD

Changing the minds of American teachers about the potential of Students of Color is not an easy task. The media works against the possibility of positive images being attributed to People of Color, but this is not a new problem in our society; it is an old problem, a very old problem. History has also made its contribution to the confusion. How it is that people cannot coexist without power struggles is probably more related to the fact that we are simply a higher level of animal and that we have imposed upon ourselves sets of laws and morals as ways to aspire to a civilized existence. Takaki (1993) reveals that fear was the driving force in the struggle to maintain dominance and whiteness for America's first settlers. Although it is clear that the newly arrived settlers struggled to maintain identity, as well as their assumed power, they could never have survived without the help of Native American Indians. Indentured servants, White and Black, found common ground, but their continued union caused intense fear to rise in the breasts of Whites – of their unions, Black babies were born. Yesterday we struggled with identity and tried to gain footing as a nation of people, emerging from different shores, but today we struggle with the remnants of those divisive struggles. The end result is the heaviness of racism and separatism that has settled into our educational systems.

Every word, gesture, and facial expression between student and teacher in a classroom signifies a lasting impression, a silent message, paving the way for a permanent change in affect and/or demeanor. Parents and pupils want to believe that teachers, instructors, and professors leave their racism at the threshold of the classroom, but racism continues to raise its head and infect the educational process. The world is perceived through lived experiences, sensory perception, and consciousness, and these experiences systematically trigger subconscious predictions that cause people to very quickly, right or wrong, draw inferences from previous look-alike situations. People in general do not always know exactly why certain stimuli elicit varied responses; they do not understand how these responses, which seem to be automatic, are prompted by their own consciousness. Black students, if given the opportunity, can provide scenarios related to encounters with teachers/instructors/professors and explain how those encounters have systematically impaired (temporarily or permanently) their abilities to achieve and successfully matriculate.

Studying human consciousness, self-awareness, and existence helps to unlock the meanings of occurrences responsible for guiding responses or reactions to others. Students with little or no recourse internalize negative experiences that determine future relationships, and those negative experiences, particularly in the case of students and teachers, seriously impact success or failure in the classroom. Reactions are guided by previous experiences that rest just below the surface of our psyches, our consciousness, waiting to be re-lived. Jung (1959) suggests that we are all part of a collective unconscious—behaviors are connected to the same types of behaviors in the universe. The deeper meaning of the ingenious way that racism filters into a classroom via text, curriculum, or coded lecture is often glossed over, passed off as misunderstanding or not discussed at all.

Students often stop short of higher education goals because of a lack of guidance, but sometimes they are discouraged by their teachers. Assumed socio-economic status and skin color contribute to a playground that cannot be leveled unless all educators are willing to let go of old ideas. Encounters in the classroom with educators owing to power imposed on students can result in the buildup of frustration that manifests itself as anger. The anger is an "expected" outcome associated with the stereotype that all Black people are angry and hostile. The inability of these students to express themselves because they are silenced or made to feel a level of discomfort, prevents them from participating in class discussions or other activities; this silencing can result in outbursts that are blamed on students who are deemed "out of control." These students may leave one classroom and enter the next one filled with frustration, carrying the sting of affronts or threats, and looking for a place to unload.

Teacher training programs often shape the ways that teachers perceive Students of Color, especially Black students. Howard (1990) in *Getting Smart: The Social Contract of Intelligence* argues that the obstruction lies at the most fundamental level of our thinking about people and their capabilities (p. 1). But how are these ideas formed? The influence of psychoanalytical theories on teacher training programs may be the culprit. For example, Vygotsky's (1978) Zone of Proximal Development carries a great deal of weight; it is defined as - the distance between the actual development level as determined by independent problem solving and the level of potential development as determined through problem solving under adult guidance or in collaboration with more capable peers (p. 86). Vygotsky's theory strongly suggests that children can only function well in their own environments, but outside of these environments they will fail. Ideas such as this can remain rigidly implanted in the minds of White professionals, emerging as a guideline to follow in establishing levels of expectation. In a general sense, what is being said is that not all children are capable of achieving at the same level. By comparison, Chinese and Japanese school systems assure that children are prepared to learn before they enter school, proving that parental intervention and early introduction to the skill and discipline of sitting still and listening, as well as early learning preparation extended to all children equally will result in equality in education and better opportunities for all. Children who have older siblings and parents who assist their learning process or "teach" them by reading or showing by example also have advantages. But what has a tendency to happen in American schools is that the inability to achieve is closely related to the achievement of White children, and then a concentrated effort is made early on to separate children into groups, to label them.

The stigma placed on Children of Color can come from all directions—family, peers, teachers, and others. The assumption is made that children who do not have advantages are Black, "At Risk," and will *never* be able to achieve as well as Whites, so the expectations are very low and less effort is put forth to ensure that achievement is possible. Students who know they are not being treated equally naturally rebel and act out. Learning cannot take place in an environment where teachers frustrate and thwart efforts instead of teaching, so in the end, the teachers' conclusion that these children are not capable of learning at the same level as their White counterparts is justified.

But if the children are strong enough, owing to support systems at home and after school programs, they will not necessarily succumb to self-hatred, which is often a result of dehumanization in the classroom. Although "dehumanizing" may seem a strong term, it is appropriate because once an educator perceives a child as uneducable, the child is not placed in the same category as other children and is not afforded the same opportunities. Children need tough skin in order to survive what society says about them. Educators often mention Vygotsky (1978) and the theory of the Zone of Proximal Development when justifying the classification of students. The results are low expectations for some and high expectations for others.

Students know, intuitively, the difference between encouragement and disparagement. When young children are placed in reading groups in first grade, the group names play an important role in the way they perceive themselves in the classroom, the way they are perceived by their peers, and the way they will be perceived by future teachers in accordance with reference to the cumulative file wherein notes are placed. The "Eagles" group will experience a higher level of respect and self-esteem than the "Monkeys," the group that will experience ridicule and shame, resulting in poor performance. In addition, Black children seated in the back rows of classrooms are the direct result of a teacher's indoctrination into the society in which he or she lives. It is also true that Students of Color who sit in the front row of a classroom may run the risk of experiencing a state of invisibility when attempting to participate in classroom discussions; the invisible raised, waving hand syndrome. Black students at all levels of education given the opportunity can recall and report incidents that include being ignored or ridiculed in front of a classroom. They can speak to the lack of validation and the embarassment of being ignored when raising their hands to respond to questions.

Returning to a discussion of the influences of psychoanalytical writers, Erikson (1950), an influential psychologist who identified the Psychosocial Stages of Development, included in his book, *Identity and Society*, a chapter titled "Black Identity." It is mentioned here because the book is still in print and available through bookstores and online. The concepts therein can be studied and embraced by educators along with other psychoanalytical theories that shape minds and prepare teachers for leadership in cur-

POEMS, MAXIMS & EXTENDED THOUGHTS

riculum development in all disciplines of education, including psychology. Although some may argue that a misreading of Erikson has occurred, it is important to look closely at the implications of his words. The residual effects of teachings that undermine the ability of Black students to excel in education are negative and seriously impact the multiple ways that White teachers perceive Black students. How does one battle the lasting impressions of Erikson whose text, *Black Identity,* fails to support even the remotest possibility that Black identify can be positive:

> Negro babies often receive sensual satisfaction, which provides them with enough oral and sensory surplus for a lifetime, as clearly betrayed in the way they move, laugh, talk, and sing. Their forced symbiosis with the feudal south capitalized on this oral sensory treasure and helped to guild a slave's identity: mild, submissive, dependent, somewhat querulous, but always ready to serve, with occasional empathy and childlike wisdom. But underneath a dangerous split occurred. The Negro's unavoidable identification with the dominant race, and the need of the master race to protect its identity against the very sensual and oral temptations from the race held to be inferior (whence came their mammies), established in both groups an association: light-clean-white, and dark-dirty-dumb-nigger. (pp. 241–242)

Erikson attributes slavery's success to a superimposed "true identity" that could not be suppressed, which strongly suggests that Black people were always slaves, as if this were their rightful position in life at birth. He implants unforgettable images into the minds of his readers, images easily prompted by a Black face.

By comparison, Mahler, Pine, and Bergman (1975) in *The Psychological Birth of the Human Infant,* describe infants in the "subphase" of individuation—the period that Erikson alludes to and attributes only to Black infants, as follows:

> We can watch the infant molding to the mother's body and distancing from it with his trunk; we can watch him handle transitional objects. Hoffer emphasized the importance of touch (1949, 1950a. 1050b) in the boundary-formation process as well as the importance of libidinization of the infant's body by the mother. Greenacre emphasizes the "approximation of a sense of oneness by dint of the warm body of mother or nurse [which]

represents a relatively small degree of difference in temperature, smell, resilience" . . . One would expect that when inner pleasure, due to safe anchorage within the symbiotic orbit continues and pleasure in the maturationally increasing outer sensory perception stimulates outward-directed attention cathexis, these two forms of attention cathexis can oscillate freely . . . the result should be an optimal symbiotic state, out of which smooth differentiation can take place. (p. 53)

While Erikson paints a negative and "dark" picture, Mahler et al. present a review of a natural process, a mother loving and caring for a breast-feeding infant. In response to Erikson's characterization of the relationship between the Black infant and his mother, Husserl (1970) might respond in this way:

> . . . In these we discover as a common circumstance the fact that certain objects or states of affairs of whose reality someone has actual knowledge indicate to him the reality of certain other objects or states of affairs, in the sense that his belief in the reality of the one is experienced through (though not at all evidently) as motivating a belief or surmise in the reality of the other. (p.184)

Reading material is the single most important introduction to the written word. The Basal readers of 1950s, such as the *Dick, Jane, and Sally* primers were an integral part of primary education. These short readers served to build vocabularies by employing "sight words" and provided a vision of an accepted world, a world without People of Color; the words represented only half of what Black students and other Students of Color learned. Images of Blackness throughout the world were relegated to such stories as *Little Black Sambo, The Adventures of Huckleberry Finn*, and *Uncle Tom's Cabin*. Blacks were presented as buffoons, functional illiterates, slaves—shuffling, reactionary puppets whose strings were held and pulled by Whites. These images were presented globally and still hold a great deal of power.

The stage was preset for separation and differences in families that did not *match* Dick, Jane, and Sally's family. Black families were literally "painted" into the primers in the late 1970s, but it was too late to correct the damage already done by other texts and media. These images were unrecognizable as Black families. Even in today's world, the stories and images found in *Little Black Sambo, The Adventures of Huckleberry Finn*, and others remain

POEMS, MAXIMS & EXTENDED THOUGHTS

as favorites in American literature, reminding some readers of their assumed place in the American society.

Children are vulnerable as they enter pre-school and continue on through primary and secondary school settings. As consciousness begins to function in the external world children begin to recognize faces, sounds, and sensations, and then learn to read, write, and compute; persuasive and influential messages begin to shape them. As maturation occurs, youths are further exposed to messages embedded in texts and media, such as the subtle messages that denigrate specific ethnic groups. When youths are labeled "minority," assumptions accompany that definition. Wirth (1945) in *The Problem of Minority Groups*, defined the term "minority" as follows:

> A group of people who, because of physical or cultural characteristics, are singled out from others in society in which they live for differential and unequal treatment, and who therefore regard themselves as objects of collective discriminations . . . Minority status carries with it the exclusion from full participation in the life of the society. (p. 347)

A young person easily becomes a fabrication of the environment, learning to respond to and treating others well or poorly based on programmed behavior. The damage is done when reactions and responses, automatic or calculated, change the lives of givers and receivers.

Educational processes across the disciplines show that little or no effort is ever made to hide the factors that support social stratification, dividing levels of power and keeping specific ethnic groups on the lower wrung of society. Although some may argue that the teacher/student dyad is completely different than that of client and therapist, the dynamics are basically the same. Ridley (1995) defines cultural counter transference, using Sigmund Freud's conceptualization:

> Counter transference refers to the emotional reactions of therapists, which are projected onto clients. These reactions are similar to previous reactions to someone other than the client – a person outside of therapy with whom the counselor has had an intense emotional experience. The reactions are caused by the therapist's anxiety. The failure of these counselors to resolve their feelings results in a misperception of the client. (p. 71)

This relationship, communication practice, and process can be applied to the teacher/student dyad; the implications are far reaching and damaging. Jones (1985) comments specifically on how therapists counter transfer onto Black clients:

> Any client [student] can invoke in a therapist [teacher] an unhelpful emotional response; what is noteworthy for this discussion is that it appears that Black patients [students] may evoke more complicated counter transference reactions and more frequently. The reason for this seems to be that social images of Blacks [students] still make them easier targets for therapists' [teachers'] projections and that the culturally different client [student] provides more opportunities for emphatic failures. (p. 178)

Stereotypes are included in the repertoire during indoctrination, so as the person undergoing indoctrination is raised, educated, and prepared professionally (disciplined) to promote education or psychology, personality and perception develop and stabilize. Education teaches skills, values, attitudes, and division. The teacher, harboring old wounds, can transfer those negative feelings to the student, impacting the student forever even thwarting his or her ability to gain knowledge and to engage in learning through the classroom experience. When the student responds in a negative fashion, the teacher believes that his or her suspicions about the student are justified. The old adage "You can't teach an old dog new tricks," is important when people have established belief systems and are not open to new possibilities or ways of "seeing" and "learning" that the student is not always at fault. Sometimes the problem rests with the teacher.

Ridley (1995) argues that the non-white client [student] is reacting strongly to the *negative projections* (racist attitudes and behaviors) of the therapist [teacher]. Although the reactions of the client [student] are justified, the therapist [teacher] tends to misinterpret the response and proceeds to label the client [student] as pathological. This is called "pseudo transference." The process of labeling in a school or college setting can result in dismissal, relegation to the back of the room, expulsion, or a random diagnosis of Attention Deficit Disorder (ADD). The bottom line is that the student suffers, and the teacher is left to do even more damage and never having to address his or her own issues. Once an individual is conditioned to sense or experience a specific trigger, perception guides the resulting response. Marleau-Ponty (1962) observes,

POEMS, MAXIMS & EXTENDED THOUGHTS

The light of a candle changes its appearance for a child; after a burn, it stops attracting the child's hand and becomes literally repulsive . . . Vision is already inhibited by meaning (sens) which gives it a function in the spectacle of the world and in our existence. (p. 61)

Perception plays an important role in initial and future encounters with a stimulus. People observing the same incident can interpret the scene in various ways. Unfortunately, this is a common occurrence when people who are heavily influenced to think negatively of others. Delpit (1995), author of *Other People's Children*, provides an example a scenario observed by a White woman whose assessment of and comments about the situation are equally disturbing.

Charles is a three-year-old African American boy who likes a little White girl in his nursery school class. Like most three-year-olds, his affection is expressed as much with hugs as with hits. One morning I notice that Charles has been hovering around Kelly, his special friend. He grabs her from behind and tries to give her a bear hug. When she protests, the teacher tells him to stop. A short time later he returns to her table to kiss her on the cheek. She protests again and the teacher puts him in time-out. I comment to the teacher with a smile that Charles certainly seems to have a little crush on Kelly. She frowns and replies that his behavior is *"way out of line."* She continues with disgust in her voice, *"Sometimes what he does just looks like lust."* (p. xii)

Something in this teacher's training, indoctrination, life experiences, and or family experience influenced her object-relationship with Black children. She cannot see Charles as an innocent, affectionate three-year-old; she sees him as lustful in his approach to the little White girl. She ensures that the show of affection is met with punishment, which will confuse Charles, who is led to believe that he has done something wrong. The lesson the teacher intends is that he should not show affection to White girls.

Johnson (1993), in *A Culturally Sensitive Approach to Therapy with Children*, argues that most people do not routinely assess their reactions to different situations and different people to determine their biases and prejudices. This assessment process is not one that is typically present in many people's minds on an ongoing basis. However, it is an important process on the road to becoming culturally sensitive . . . there are various ways to work on counter transference issues regarding other cultures (p. 73). Johnson goes on to suggest that internal reactions to ethnic jokes might be a clue to one's sensitivity to other cultures. The powerful truth is that people who are not usually the brunt of jokes and/or who are not deemed "invisible" in the classroom do not often think of themselves as "completely out of line" in their assumptions about or failure to validate others.

Morrison (1992) in her essay *The Kindness of Sharks* makes an important point about the way textbooks and other literatures serve to instruct beyond the printed word. She describes the "namelessness" of Blacks in literature by citing an Ernest Hemingway novel, *To Have and Have Not*. Morrison explains:

> Harry says "Wesley" when speaking to the Black man in direct dialogue; Hemingway writes "nigger" when as narrator he refers to him. Needless to report, this Black man is never identified as one (except in Hemmingway's own mind). Part two reserves and repeats the word "man" for Harry. The spatial and conceptual difference is marked by the shortcut that the term "nigger" allows, with all of its color and caste implications. The term occupies a territory between man and animal and thus withholds specificity even while marking it. This Black character either does not speak (as a "nigger" he is silent) or speaks in very legislated and manipulated ways (as a "Wesley" his speech serves Harry's needs). Enforcing the silence of the "nigger" proves problematic in the action-narrative and requires Hemingway some strenuous measures. (p. 71)

Literature does its part in a sophisticated way to continue indoctrinating the *educated mind* so that it will remember who belongs in which place. The Black man cannot be a man; he is a "nigger" when referred to indirectly. This suggests that our society has two voices, an open voice and one that speaks under the breath.

A Black student reading *To Have And Have Not* can: 1) sit through the process, contracting muscles involuntarily during open discussions; 2) drop the class in total frustration, remarking internally how little times have changed; or, 3) speak out and run the risk of failing or being disciplined. His or her motivation to continue can be easily thwarted. Husserl (1970) advises that there can be no meaning if what is offered, as a sign does not connote meaning to the target recipient. He argues, "A thing is only properly an indication if and where it, in fact, serves to indicate something to some thinking being" (p. 185). The trigger then cannot ignite a response if the recipient does not recognize the attack, or if the recipient is tough enough not to absorb it.

Eagan (1992) in his book *The Educated Mind*, argues that he has a persuasive purpose, so he has not tried to highlight the virtues of alternative general schemes, but in teaching [about the educated mind] to a university class he would explore in particular other developmental schemes, such as those of Piaget, Vygotsky, and Erikson . . . drawing attention to the dimensions of cultural and/or individual development about which they enhance our understanding. And further, he says that he would try to make clear that these varied implications from them [Piaget, Vygotsky, and Erikson] should not be seen so much as to-the-death competitions for the truth but rather as comparatively useful aids in understanding the processes to which they refer (p. 270). Teachers who detect the *code*, accept the rhetoric, and are indoctrinated in a manner that leads to the belief that Blacks cannot achieve. Undermining the education of Black students is accomplished in several ways: Treat the students as if they are invisible; pay little or no attention to their abilities; make a concentrated effort not to validate these students in the open classroom; and/or, denigrate their ethnicity in the presence of classmates.

Teachers are responsible for reshaping skills and values, and they also have the power to support students along the way to success while failing others. Clearly, if teachers are heavily influenced to believe that only certain children have the innate ability to succeed academically while others should not be encouraged, then those teachers without intervention for the sake of the students exposed to them will become the deciding factors for the future of those students.

Silent forces are working when a line in a textbook reveals a casually inserted racial epithet that calls up images and ideas and arouses negative emotions that only the group it undermines feels on a visceral level while others notice and cringe or shrug, but do not comment. Even more disturbing is the fact that the writings of some authors are misinterpreted and then employed to support ideas for which there have never been viable connections. Teachers who care to do so should take on the responsibility of modeling positive behavior and incorporating critical thinking into every instructional process in an effort to make classrooms safe for discussion about inequality and the perpetuation of myths about People of Color.

Students of today are tomorrow's adults; Students of Color are in serious danger. Many strategic planning meetings rally around the *abstract idea* of achieving equality while focusing on equity, and no one to date can agree on the correct approach to leveling the imaginary playing field of education or closing the widening abyss of achievement between Black and White students. Certainly, we should start with the "human" aspect of the problem, those who are strategically placed at every level of education to encourage some students and to thwart the efforts of others. Discussions around personal values and beliefs are difficult because people often deny that there is something going on beneath the surface of their responses to others.

Strategic planning for primary, secondary, and post-secondary curriculum must promote, embrace, and model diversity. Borrowing a checklist of strategies from Rachel Martin's (2001) *Listen Up: Reinventing Ourselves As Teachers and Students,* the following represents a "must add" list for future curriculum standards:

- Recognize that complexity is a pedagogical resource
- Value hunches over certainties
- Move from the known to the unknown
- Position everyone as smart
- Encourage risk taking
- Decrease anxiety
- Recognize the social nature of learning
- Recognize that motivation comes through comment not correction
- Recognize that specific structures of language emerge in meaningful contexts
- Affirm cultural diversity
- Value home languages
- Create an environment in which everyone feels in his/ her element

Teachers, instructors, and professors hold very special places at the head of classrooms, and these positions should be held in the highest regard because of the many lives these professionals influence. In the words of Shor (1987), "The liberating classroom . . . challenges the student to unveil the actual manipulation and myths in society. In that unveiling, we change our understanding of reality, our perceptions" (p. 172). We have a distance to travel to right the wrongs perpetrated against the young, but if we are careful and do not stray from the path, we will arrive and do our best work for the sake of the future.

POEMS, MAXIMS & EXTENDED THOUGHTS

REFERENCES

Delpit, L. (1995). *Other people's children: Cultural conflict in the classroom.* New York: The New Press.

Egan, K. (1992). *The educated mind: New cognitive tools to shape our understanding.* Chicago: The University of Chicago Press.

Erikson, E. H. (1950). *Identity and society.* New York: W.W. Norton & Company.

Howard, J. (1990). *Getting smart: The social construction of intelligence.* The Efficacy Institute, Inc. (pp. 1–17).

Husserl, E. (1970). *Logical investigations* (vol. 1). London, EG: Routledge Classics.

Johnson, M. (1993). A culturally sensitive approach to therapy with children. In C. Brems (Ed.), *A comprehensive guide to child psychotherapy* (pp. 68–94). Boston, MA: Allyn & Bacon.

Jones, E. E. (1985). Psychotherapy and counseling with black clients. In P. Pedersen (Ed.), *Handbook of cross-cultural counseling and therapy* (pp. 173–179). Westport, CT: Greenwood Press.

Jung, C. G. (1978). *Aion: Researches into the phenomenology of the self* (2nd ed.). Princeton, NJ: Princeton University Press.

Mahler, M., Pine, F., & Bergman, A. (1979). *The psychological birth of the human infant: Symbiosis and individuation.* New York: Basic Books.

Martin, R. (2001). *Listen up: Reinventing ourselves as teachers and students.* Portsmouth, NH: Boynton/Cook Publishing, Inc.

Morrison, T. (1992). *Playing in the dark.* Cambridge, MA: Harvard University Press.

Ponty, M. (1945). *Phenomenology of perception.* New York: Rutledge Classics

Ridley, C. R. (1995). *Overcoming unintentional racism in counseling and therapy: A practitioner's guide to intentional intervention.* London, EG: Sage Publications.

Shor, I., & Freire, P. (1987). *A pedagogy for liberation: Dialogues on transforming education.* South Hadley, MA: Bergin & Garvey.

Takaki, R. (1993). *A different mirror.* New York: Little Brown.

Vygotsky, L. (1978). *Mind in society: The development of higher psychological processes.* Cambridge, MA: Harvard University Press.

Wirt, L. (1945). The problem of minority groups. In R. Linton (Ed.), *The science of man in the world crisis* (pp. 347–372). New York: Colombia University Press.

MARGINALITY: PROMOTION OF THE THEORY AND USE OF THE LABEL

"The crazy part of my life even though it was devastating, was the beginning of what I believed was a consistent and growing genocidal level of destruction predicate on the premise that there are marginalized youth with no jobs or future, and these youth, therefore, are expendable." (Luis Rodriguez, 1993)

According to a review of the literature on marginality theory, the concept of marginality has a long tradition in sociology: the theory of marginality holds that developmental processes, as they pertain to the socialization of individuals, are not the same for all members of a society (Grant & Breese 1997). In the journal article "Marginality Theory and the African American Student," two White middle-class sociologists, Grant and Breese (1997) present the results of their study undertaken to determine the ways in which African American Students react to their state of marginality. The study concludes that these students construct meaning related to their state of marginality, and this construction of meaning is responsible for the lack of retention and low graduation rate for African American students on college campuses. Further, marginality, as it relates to African American students, is a sociological tradition, a confirmed "status." The study was conducted at a midwestern state university. Grant and Breese set out to confirm reactions to the state of marginality and to determine the ways in which those reactions could be manipulated to allow African Americans to "adapt and function in concert with the 'dominant culture.'" Categories describing reactions to marginality were limited to: affected, emulative, defiant, emissarial, withdrawn, balanced, paradoxical, and uninvolved, yet the sample group did not fit neatly into those categories.

The *method* included a questionnaire designed to solicit specific answers related to life, education, and professional decisions. The control group, as previously stated, consisted of African American students from an "urban, public university." Faculty members were asked to select "likely candidates." The study concluded that the perceptions on the part of the students were responsible for their individual responses within the designated categories to their marginal legacy. If the theory of marginality is discussed and incorporated into teacher education/training courses, what chance is there that teachers will not maintain the concept and apply it, sometimes unwittingly, to Students of Color? Should educators be concerned about a theory that is driving the education of African American youth? Here is an example of marginalization at work: Johnny still can't read or write well, but he is receiving "B's" on his papers. Why is the teacher passing him? Is the teacher not willing to spend the extra time with Johnny to bring him up to speed? What does this mean? Suppose Mary is rebelling now because she got all "A's" and "B's" last semester, and her new teacher is pushing her to actually perform at the A and B levels. Are the students being marginalized? According to Grant and Breese, both students are *marginal*; both students are from a *subculture*; both students are *under-class, low-class, minorities*; both students are African American. The power of the words drives the perception.

Definitions are woven into the fabric of the label. The word "marginal" is commonly employed in conversations about Blacks and education. Seized and embraced by educators, sociologists, anthropologists, psychologists, and society at large, the term is freely used—without explanation, assuming that the reader knows what is being referenced—in literature and journal articles in many fields of study, causing major problems: 1) The word "marginal" labels groups, which influences the way members are treated and taught. 2) Educators experience difficulties getting beyond the labels and into pedagogy. 3) Looming somewhere in a mystical state is the idea that the purpose of education is to educate the *brightest and the best* while preparing the marginal for the workplace. 4) Conceptualization and implementation of multicultural education redirects the focus away from the *brightest and the best*. And 5) marginalization maintains the status quo. Examine the fabric of the word "marginal," and make note of the way the meaning promotes the idea that the individual who is labeled as such has no possible means of becoming an integral part of society; his or her potential is deemed not good enough to spend time cultivating.

> Marginal: **adjective, noun, & verb** . . . 1. written or printed in the margin of a page or sheet (marginal notes). 2. Pertaining to an edge, border, or boundary: situated at or affecting the extreme edge of an area, body, etc.: not central . . . excluded from or existing outside the mainstream of society, a group, or a school of thought. (Stevenson, 2007, p. 1706)

Marginalization singles individuals out to be treated differently, to be responded to differently, and to be educated differently. Grant and Breese surveyed 23 Black college students who revealed that they were completely aware of the ways they were being treated in college [none acknowledged or mentioned marginalization]; many developed ways of coping so that they would not be prevented from getting the education they had come for. Grant and Breese's study found that students did not, in fact, respond as they were expected to.

While none of the students responded in the categories of *affected* or *emulative*, which would include hypersensitivity and denial of one's race, respectively, four of the students met criteria for defiant. The *defiant* category is described as blaming the establishment or system for individual failure. Students responding in this category were not typically overtly violent. In one example, the student preferred being alone, focusing on personal problems, and dropping any class that presented too much of a problem (Grant & Breese, 1997). Another student chose to use her knowledge of the system and history to promote herself as "Little Malcolm." She was known and respected by her peers and worked for the Office of Minority Affairs to help students resolve conflict within the college's system. In this case, since the respondent was working within the system, she was connected and made progress, maintaining a 3.5 GPA. Still another student learned to *work the system* aided by two White friends. According to Grant and Breese, this association gave her the chance to participate in actively confronting a racial issue with the Office of Minority Affairs, but was still considered *defiant* because she sought to change the system.

To demonstrate how words can be manipulated, review the first paragraph of the article in question; it includes a reference to bell hooks (1992) *Black Looks*:

> Research has demonstrated that the retention and graduation rates for African American students are relatively low (Bruno 1988: Doob 1996) and that social factors, especially the subjective experience of marginality, are strongly related to retention and graduation (Giles-Gee 1989). As hooks noted, "I learned as a child that to be 'safe,' it was important to recognize the power of whiteness, even to fear it, and to avoid encounter" (1992:175) -- in essence, to remain marginal in society. (Grant & Breese, 1997, p. 192)

Taken out of context, the hooks quote is employed to suggest that hooks buys into the notion of marginality as it is presented in the study, but a

POEMS, MAXIMS & EXTENDED THOUGHTS

closer look at the quote in its intended context reveals a completely different message. In the actual quote, hooks (1992) states:

> In the absence of the reality of whiteness, I learned as a child that to be 'safe,' it was important to recognize the power of whiteness, even to fear it, and to avoid encounter. There was nothing terrifying about the sharing of this knowledge as a survival strategy. The terror was made real only when I journeyed from the black side of town to a predominantly white area near my grandmother's house. I had to pass through this area to reach her place. (p. 175)

Herein, hooks is talking about the experience in her own neighborhood. As the paragraph continues, it is clear that hooks is describing the types of looks her presence prompted when walking through the neighborhood where "poor white trash" lived. She describes "the journey across town":

> It was a movement away from the segregated blackness of our community into a poor white neighborhood. I remember the fear, being scared to walk to Baba's, our grandmother's house, because we would have to pass that terrifying whiteness -- those white faces on the porches staring us down with hate. Even when empty or vacant those porches seemed to say *danger*, you do not belong here, you are not safe. (p. 175)

Further, hooks links the idea of terror to the concept of whiteness, having more to do with the environment and the predicament of Whites caught up in the separation of classes: upper class Whites, middle class Whites, poor Whites, and poor White trash; bell hooks is referencing a lifestyle where the anger of poor Whites was even worse than that of other categories of whiteness because no matter how rich or poor Blacks were, they were never considered better than the lowest class of whiteness, poor White trash. And those who fell into the category of poor White trash were meaner and more willing to take action—they had nothing to lose. Review of the hooks piece led me to research other books to find references to marginality that better fit the results of the study—the ways that educators experience the marginality of students. I found that Delpit's (1995) *Other People's Children*, included several useful cases.

Delpit (1993) stated:

> I further believe that to act as if power does not exist is to en-
> sure that the power status quo remains the same. To imply to
> children or adults (but of course the adults won't believe you
> anyway) that it doesn't matter how you talk or how you write is
> to ensure their ultimate failure. (p. 93)

Addressing the many ways in which the notion of marginality is delivered
to students, Delpit (1993) reminds us,

> To deny a student entry under the notion of upholding stan-
> dards is to blame the victim for the crime. We cannot justifi-
> ably enlist exclusionary standards when the reason this student
> lacked the skills demanded was poor teaching at the best and
> racism at the worst . . . to bring a student into a program and
> pass her through without attending to obvious deficits in the
> codes needed for her to function effectively, a teacher is equally
> criminal -- for though we may assuage our own consciences for
> not participating in victim blaming, she will surely be accused
> and convicted as soon as she leaves the university. (p. 38)

Delpit discusses a Native Alaskan woman's experience in a teacher edu-
cation program. This young woman was not initially given the assistance
needed to improve her writing skills and may have gone on to fail had it not
been for Delpit's' assistance.

The Grant and Breese (1997) study employed a qualitative research model.
In this case, the students did not fit neatly into each slot, and Grant and
Breese discovered that students responded and conducted themselves in
accordance with their individual and collective knowledge of the educa-
tional process and the ways they experienced their environment, the ways
they were treated by their teachers and peers, not specifically the manip-
ulation of perceived marginality. This article reminded me of the ways in
which propaganda, veiled hints, myths, half-truths, and lies find their way
into the mainstream of language, culture, and education through the repe-
tition of words. Safely implanted, words and sentiments thrive and become
permanent ways of thinking that unwittingly or with intention influence
the ways that people think about and respond to others both consciously
and subconsciously. Words guide the constructs of conversation, literature,

media, theory, and pedagogy. If the "likely candidates" are selected and identified as "marginal" by a people who are presently struggling to maintain their alleged position of prestige and power, how can the results be anything other than a confirmation of marginality? The theory of marginality assures White middle-class sociologists and ethnographers a level of safety.

The study has its strengths and weaknesses, but educators - to ensure that they are introduced to how biased a seemingly unbiased study can be, to see how a label can be applied and made to fit even when the criteria are not met - should read it. The more one learns, the more one understands how myths, stereotypes, and the like are perpetuated—through literature, psychology, sociology, anthropology, science, and a myriad of other disciplines. One may also grow to understand that textbooks teach whatever story the so-called *dominant culture* wants to tell, and this situation is not likely to change in the near future.

REFERENCES

Bartholomae, D., & Petrosky, A. (1986). *Facts, artifacts, and counteracts: Theory and method for a reading and writing course.* Portsmouth, NH: Boynton/Cook Publishers.

Delpit, L. (1995). *Other people's children: Cultural conflict in the classroom.* New York: The New York Press.

Egan, K. (1997). *The educated mind: How cognitive tools shape our understanding.* Chicago: University of Chicago Press.

Erikson, E. (1986). *Identify youth and crisis.* New York: W.W. Norton & Company.

Grant, G., & Breese, J. (1997). Marginality theory and the African American student. *Sociology of Education,* 70 (July): 192–205.

Hoggart, R. (2000). *The uses of literacy.* New Brunswick, NJ: Transaction Publishers.

hooks, b. (1992). *Black looks.* Boston: South End Press.

Kutz, E., Groden, S., & Zamel, V. (1993). *The discovery of competence: Teaching and learning with diverse student writers.* Portsmouth, NH: Boynton/Cook Publishers.

Rimstead, R. (1995). Between theories and anti-theories: Moving toward marginal women's subjectivities. *Women's Studies Quarterly,* 23: 199–218.

Rodriguez, L. (1993). *Always running*. New York: Simon and Schuster.

Shaughnessy, M. (1977). *Errors and expectations: A guide for the teacher of basic writing*. New York: Oxford University Press.

Smith, B. (2000, September). Marginalized youth, delinquency, and education: the need for critical-interpretive research. *The Urban Review*, 32(3): 293–312.

Stevenson, A. (Ed.). (2007). *Shorter Oxford English dictionary on historical principles* (6th ed., vol. 1). New York: Oxford University Press.

POEMS, MAXIMS & EXTENDED THOUGHTS

Exercise

5

The two writings "Exploring the Written Word" and "Marginality: Promotion of the Theory and Use of the Label" represent the use of research and the incorporation of the writings and research of others.

PART I: Reread and annotate "Exploring the Written Word." Write a rebuttal regarding what you find there—whatever your interpretation is, it is welcome and will be respected. Approach the writing with the intent to dissect it, to deconstruct it—think critically. Ask and answer the questions: What is the writer's purpose? What position does the writer take (the argument)? What is the evidence? Do you agree? Disagree?

PART II: Research Task:

Step I: Find at minimum six sources (studies, periodicals/journals, peer-reviewed articles, books, advertisements) that explore or demonstrate the ways that writing can erupt and produce microaggressions, and/or influence readers to think, feel, and act in specific ways. List the names of sources here, and begin creating a Works Cited page (for Modern Language Association style) or References page (for American Psychological Association style) in accordance with the extended writing instructions provided by your professor.

Sources:

1.

2.

3.

4.

5.

6.

Step II: Create an annotated bibliography.

Step III: Write a thesis statement.

Step IV: Outline the research.

Step V: Write the research paper.

The research paper will develop over several drafts (a timeline will be provided).

Attach this worksheet and any additional pages to your final project.

Exercise

6

PART I: Reread and annotate "Marginality: Promotion of the Theory and Use of the Label." Write a rebuttal regarding what you find there—whatever your interpretation is, it is welcome and will be respected. Approach the writing with the intent to dissect it, to deconstruct it. Ask and answer the questions: What is the writer's purpose? What position does the writer take (the argument)? What roles do stereotyping and labeling play in the formation of ideas and concepts? What is the evidence? Do you agree? Disagree?

PART II:

Research Task:

Step I: Find at minimum six sources (studies, periodicals/journals, peer-reviewed articles, books, advertisements) that explore or demonstrate the ways that labeling can create perceptions of others. List sources here, and begin creating a Works Cited page (for Modern Language Association style) or References page (for American Psychological Association style) in accordance with the extended writing instructions provided by your professor.

Sources:

1.

2.

3.

4.

5.

6.

Step II: Create an annotated bibliography.

Step III: Write a thesis statement.

Step IV: Outline the research.

Step V: Write the research paper.

The research paper will develop over several drafts (a timeline will be provided).

Attach this worksheet and any additional pages to your final project.

POEMS, MAXIMS & EXTENDED THOUGHTS